Kathy —

Keep seek

Sharon Ellis

Our Passover Lamb

(Plus miscellaneous Bible studies at end of book)

WESTBOW
PRESS®
A DIVISION OF THOMAS NELSON
& ZONDERVAN

Copyright © 2018 Sharon Ellis.

All rights reserved. No part of this book may be used or reproduced by any means,
graphic, electronic, or mechanical, including photocopying, recording, taping or
by any information storage retrieval system without the written permission of the
author except in the case of brief quotations embodied in critical articles and reviews.

WestBow Press books may be ordered through booksellers or by contacting:

WestBow Press
A Division of Thomas Nelson & Zondervan
1663 Liberty Drive
Bloomington, IN 47403
www.westbowpress.com
1 (866) 928-1240

Because of the dynamic nature of the Internet, any web addresses or
links contained in this book may have changed since publication and
may no longer be valid. The views expressed in this work are solely those
of the author and do not necessarily reflect the views of the publisher,
and the publisher hereby disclaims any responsibility for them.

Any people depicted in stock imagery provided by Getty Images are
models, and such images are being used for illustrative purposes only.
Certain stock imagery © Getty Images.

THE HOLY BIBLE, NEW INTERNATIONAL VERSION®,
NIV® Copyright © 1973, 1978, 1984, 2011 by Biblica, Inc.®
Used by permission. All rights reserved worldwide.

ISBN: 978-1-9736-3335-8 (sc)
ISBN: 978-1-9736-3334-1 (e)

Print information available on the last page.

WestBow Press rev. date: 9/28/2018

This is a compilation of the four gospels into one story of Christ's last days on earth. My original purpose was to combine the words of each day so families could read from it daily on the week before Easter.

Then I noticed that the readings showed how
Jesus perfectly fulfilled being ...

Our Passover Lamb

... in order to pay for our sins. Then that fact became the real story!

<u>NOTES:</u>

The New International Version is used throughout this book.

Matthew is written in regular type,
<u>Mark</u> is underlined,
Luke is in italics, and
John is in bold type, and
my notes are in cursive.

This book is dedicated to
my Passover Lamb
in thankfulness for His paying the price for my sins,
giving me eternal life, living in my heart, and helping me each day.

I would also like to dedicate this book
to my late husband,
Harold Ellis,
who always believed in me.

Thank you to:
Dr. and Mrs. Jerry & Vicky Bawcom
who have helped me, encouraged me, and prayed for me;
Mary Roby for helping me and proofing this paper; and
Cathy L. Johnson for drawing the sketches which she
has dedicated to my late husband, **Harold Ellis.**

Contents

Jesus: Our Passover Lamb – 1 Corinthians 5:7

Most people assume Jesus was crucified on Friday, the preparation day before the weekly Sabbath; but, that doesn't fit with the Scripture concerning His crucifixion. Also, people believe that the last supper was the Passover meal. I believe the Bible to be the inerrant Word of God, and it bothered me when:

1. I read that Judas left the last supper, and the disciples thought it was because he went to buy something for the Passover.
   Why, if they had just eaten it?

2. It also bothered me that in John 18:28 – after the last supper – the Bible says

   > Then the Jews led Jesus from Caiaphas to the palace of the Roman governor. By now it was early morning, and to avoid ceremonial uncleanness the Jews did not enter the palace; they wanted to be able to eat the Passover (NIV).

   Why if they had just celebrated it?

3. It bothered me that my King James Bible I had as a young girl showed Matthew 28:1 as saying **after the Sabbaths**.
   Why was it plural?
   In my other Bibles that I have had after that time, **Sabbath** was singular. Fortunately, I now have a Greek-English New Testament. The Greek version has **Sabbaths** – also plural.
   Why?

There has to be an explanation. When I taught Sunday School years ago, I learned and taught that if something didn't seem right, keep studying to see if you can find the correct answer. I wanted to find the answers for these questions.

1

The first thing I did as I began writing this book was to divide the events of Jesus' last days into days of the week by looking for when **sundown** or **even** occurred. When I did that, it became apparent to me that Jesus was crucified on Thursday. That will be seen in the pages that follow.

I believe God led me to a book entitled **Three Days in the Grave** by Roy M. Allen. He too had questions, and – as a Bible scholar – found the answers. I will be including much from his book

The Jewish day is different from ours. It begins at sundown or even and extends to the following day through the next even. The way I tried to show that was by showing the evening portion of the day abbreviated and the next day spelled out, coming up with Fri/Saturday. This means the evening portion of the Jewish day was Friday and the daytime portion was Saturday.

There were two parts to the ceremonial Passover – first the killing of the lamb followed by the eating of the lamb. The lamb was slain late on Passover day. The eating of the lamb was done at even, meaning it was the beginning of the following day.

Besides the fact that the Jewish people had a regular, weekly Sabbath, there were also other Sabbaths set out for them in Leviticus 23 that they were to observe. For example, the 1st, 10th, 15th, and 22nd days of Nisan, as well other times during the year, were set out as **special Sabbaths**. We can see from the Sabbaths in the month of Nisan that the 10th and 15th are not a week apart, making it obvious that there were times when a **weekly Sabbath** would fall in between those **special Sabbaths**. That is what happened in the year Jesus was crucified.

That year, the Passover lamb was slain on Thursday. Then Friday was the Feast of the Passover sabbath, as well as being the preparation day for the weekly sabbath on Saturday. Here's what it looked like:

> Wed/Thursday: Passover lamb was to be slain --- Preparation Day for feast of Passover
>
> Thurs/Friday: Passover lamb eaten at even (called feast of the Passover: a sabbath day) --- Preparation Day for weekly sabbath
>
> Fri/Saturday: The weekly Sabbath

Here are the rules the Jewish people were to follow to celebrate Passover. After the exodus from Egypt, they were told, in Exodus, chapter 12, to pick a lamb without blemish from the flocks on the 10th day of Nisan. It was to be kept until the afternoon of the 14th day when it was to be killed in the evening around six o'clock before even came. The slain lamb was taken into the house, roasted whole, and then eaten that night, which would be the early hours of the 15th.

After the Passover lamb was sacrificed and by the time the lamb was cooked and ready to eat, it was the 15th. So, the 15th of Nisan was known as **the feast day** or **the feast of the Passover.** It was set aside as a **special Sabbath**. The feast was eaten at night, and none of the lamb was to remain until the following morning. If any remained, it had to be burned before daylight. The only difference to these rules came after the tabernacle was completed. At that time, the lambs were to be slain by the priests. There was a need to increase the time allowed for the slaying of the lambs because there were so many. Josephus, a Jewish historian, wrote that on one Passover 256,500 lambs were slain, so the time was extended to three o'clock in the afternoon to begin slaying the lambs. Three o'clock is the time of the going down of the sun – the time the sun begins to descend.

The Jewish people began removing the leaven in their home a day in advance because they did not want to be cut off from Israel. Even today that custom is still practiced among Jewish people. See Exodus 12:15 and 16. It says:

> For seven days you are to eat bread made without yeast.
> On the first day remove the yeast from your houses, for
> whoever eats anything with yeast in it from the first day
> through the seventh must be cut off from Israel. (NIV)

Approximately one-third of all that is written in the combined gospels relates entirely to the last days of Christ as He was crucified. That tells me it was very important --- so important that we need to study and understand what God is trying to teach us. Since Jesus was our Passover lamb, I believe He met every one of the criteria which God had set in place over 1500 years before Jesus' birth, and I hope you see that in this study. What difference does it make? I believe understanding God's word correctly adds more meaning for us. I know the event is more meaningful to me now that I see how He perfectly fulfilled the rules of being our Passover lamb. Why would He set out these exact rules in Exodus and Leviticus and then not follow them?

I have written notes at the beginning of each day to discuss what happened on that day.

Sat/**Sunday**

(Matthew 21:1-11; <u>Mark 11:1-11;</u>
Luke 19:28-44; **John 12:12-19** [NIV])

10th day of Nisan:

The Triumphal Entry, which we now call Palm Sunday, occurred on this day; the day when Jesus was chosen as the king by the crowds who cried out:

> Hosanna! Blessed is he who comes in the name of the Lord! Blessed is the coming kingdom of our father David! Hosanna in the highest! (Mark 11:9). (NIV)

It was no mere coincidence that Jesus was chosen by the people on this day because it was the 10th day of Nisan that Jesus was selected as our Passover lamb: the same day the sacrificial lamb was selected to be slain in the Temple. Just as that lamb was to be without blemish, Jesus, our Passover lamb, was without blemish – he had no sin in Him.

When the people chose Him, the chief priests and the teachers of the law heard what happened and began looking for a way to kill Him – just as the lamb chosen on the 10th day was chosen to be sacrificed on the 14th day.

As you read, you will notice the use of different fonts. Refer to the footnote at the bottom of the page if you need to in order to see which gospel the words were taken from. As you will see, Matthew is in a regular font, Mark is underlined, Luke is in italics, and John is in bold letters.

The next day as they approached Jerusalem and came to Bethphage *and Bethany at the hill called the Mount of Olives,* <u>Jesus</u>

Matthew   <u>Mark</u>   *Luke*   **John**

sent two of his disciples, saying to them, "Go to the village ahead of you and at once just as you enter you will find a donkey tied there, with her colt by her, which no one has ever ridden. Untie them and bring them here to me. If anyone says anything to you, asks you 'Why are you untying it?' tell him that the Lord needs them and will send it back here shortly, and he will send them right away."

The disciples who were sent ahead went and did as Jesus had instructed them and found a colt outside in the street just as he had told them, tied at a doorway. As they untied it, some people standing there, its owners, asked them, "What are you doing untying that colt?" They answered, "The Lord needs it," as Jesus had told them to, and the people let them go. When they brought the colt to Jesus and threw their cloaks over it, he sat on it.

The great crowd that had come for the Feast heard that Jesus was on his way to Jerusalem. They took palm branches and went out to meet him. Now the crowd that was with him had continued to spread the word that he had called Lazarus from the tomb, raising him from the dead. Many people, because they had heard that he had given this miraculous sign, went out to meet him. *As he went along,* a very large crowd spread their cloaks on the road, while others cut branches from the trees they had cut in the fields and spread them on the road.

When he came near the place where the road goes down the Mount of Olives, the whole crowd of disciples, began joyfully to praise God in loud voices for all the miracles they had seen. The crowds that went ahead of him and those that followed shouted, "Hosanna to the Son of David! Blessed is he who comes in the name of the Lord! Blessed is the coming kingdom of our father David! Hosanna in the highest! *Peace in heaven and glory in the highest!* **Blessed is the King of Israel!"**

This took place to fulfill what was spoken through the prophet: "Say to the Daughter of Zion, 'See, your king comes to you, gentle and riding on a donkey, on a colt, the foal of a donkey.'"

Matthew   Mark   *Luke*   **John**

At first his disciples did not understand all this. Only after Jesus was glorified did they realize that these things had been written about him and that they had done these things to him. *As he approached Jerusalem and saw the city, he wept over it and said, "If you, even you, had only known on this day what would bring you peace— but now it is hidden from your eyes. The days will come upon you when your enemies will build an embankment against you and encircle you and hem you in on every side. They will dash you to the ground, you and the children within your walls. They will not leave one stone on another, because you did not recognize the time of God's coming to you."*

Some of the Pharisees in the crowd said to Jesus, "Teacher, rebuke your disciples!" "I tell you," he replied, "if they keep quiet, the stones will cry out." **So the Pharisees said to one another, "See, this is getting us nowhere. Look how the whole world has gone after him!"**

When Jesus entered Jerusalem, <u>and went to the temple</u>, the whole city was stirred and asked, "Who is this?" The crowds answered, "This is Jesus, the prophet from Nazareth in Galilee."

<u>Jesus entered Jerusalem and went to the temple. He looked around at everything, but since it was already late, he went out to Bethany with the Twelve.</u>

Matthew　　　　　　<u>Mark</u>　　　　*Luke*　　　　**John**

Sun/**Monday**

(Matthew 21:12-22; <u>Mark 11:12-19</u>; *Luke 19: 45-46 [NIV]*)

11th Day of Nisan:

On this day, Jesus returned to Jerusalem and cursed the fig tree (which had always been a picture of Israel). The Jewish people knew that.

1. In Luke 13:6-9, Jesus told the parable of the barren fig tree after stating:

    > But unless you repent, you too will all perish. (Luke 13:5) (NIV)

    The listeners understood from the parable that the owner of the vineyard referred to God (see Isaiah 5:7), and the dresser is the Messiah whose public ministry lasted three and a half years.
2. Hosea 9:10 uses the fig tree to represent Israel.
3. Jeremiah received a vision of two baskets of figs, which represented Israel.

<u>The next day as they were leaving Bethany Jesus was hungry.</u> <u>Seeing in the distance a fig tree in leaf, he went to find out if it had any fruit. When he reached it, he found nothing but leaves, because it was not the season for figs. Then he said to the tree, "May no one ever eat fruit from you again." And his disciples heard him say it.</u> Immediately the tree withered. When the disciples saw this, they were amazed. "How did the fig tree wither so quickly?" they asked. Jesus replied, "I tell you the truth, if you have faith and do not doubt,

Matthew	<u>Mark</u>	*Luke*	**John**

not only can you do what was done to the fig tree, but also you can say to this mountain, 'Go, throw yourself into the sea,' and it will be done. If you believe, you will receive whatever you ask for in prayer."

On reaching Jerusalem, Jesus entered the temple area and began driving out those who were buying and selling there. He overturned the tables of the money changers and the benches of those selling doves and would not allow anyone to carry merchandise through the temple courts. And as he taught them, he said, "Is it not written, 'my house will be called a house of prayer for all nations?' But you have made it a den of robbers."

Every day he was teaching at the temple. But the chief priests and the teachers of the law *and the leaders among the* people heard this and began looking for a way to kill him, for they feared him, because the whole crowd was amazed at his teaching. *Yet they could not find any way to do it because all the people hung on his words.*

The blind and the lame came to him at the temple and Bethany, where He spent the night. He healed them. But when the chief priests and the teachers of the law saw the wonderful things he did and the children shouting in the temple area, "Hosanna to the Son of David," they were indignant. "Do you hear what these children are saying?" they asked him. "Yes," replied Jesus, "Have you never read, 'From the lips of children and infants you have ordained praise'?"

When evening came, they went out of the city to Bethany, where He spent the night.

Matthew   Mark   *Luke*   **John**

Mon/**Tuesday**

(Matthew 21:23-26:5; Mark 11:20-14:2; Luke 20:1-21:38 [NIV])

12th day of Nisan:

On this day Jesus returned to Jerusalem. The fig tree had withered. He then went to the temple courts and was teaching. The chief priests and Pharisees started asking questions in hopes that they could cause Jesus to make a mistake, and they could turn him over to the authorities to have Him killed. Later, the Sadducees tried to trick Him with questions. When Jesus left with His disciples, they asked about the temple and the signs of His coming. Jesus later states that the Passover is two days away, which would again make it on Thursday.

In the morning, as they went along, they saw the fig tree withered from the roots. Peter remembered and said to Jesus, "Rabbi, look! The fig tree you cursed has withered!"

They arrived again in Jerusalem, and while Jesus was walking in the temple courts and while he was teaching *and preaching the gospel,* the chief priests *and the teachers of the law, together with* the elders of the people came *up* to him. "By what authority are you doing these things?" they asked. "And who gave you this authority?" Jesus replied, "I will also ask you one question. If you answer me, I will tell you by what authority I am doing these things. John's baptism – where did it come from – *was it from heaven or from men? Tell me!*"

They discussed it among themselves and said, "If we say, 'From heaven,' He will ask, 'Then why didn't you believe him?' But if we say, 'From men' – we are afraid of the people; *all the people will stone us,* for they all hold that John was a prophet." So they answered Jesus, "We

---

Matthew   Mark   *Luke*   **John**

don't know *where it was from.*" Then he said, "Neither will I tell you by what authority I am doing these things.

He then began to speak to them in parables. "What do you think? There was a man who had two sons. He went to the first and said, 'Son, go and work today in the vineyard.' 'I will not,' he answered, but later he changed his mind and went. Then the father went to the other son and said the same thing. He answered, 'I will, sir,' but he did not go. Which of the two did what his father wanted? 'The first,' they answered. Jesus said to them, "I tell you the truth, the tax collectors and the prostitutes are entering the kingdom of God ahead of you. For John came to you to show you the way of righteousness, and you did not believe him, but the tax collectors and the prostitutes did. And even after you saw this, you did not repent and believe him.

"Listen to another parable: There was a landowner who planted a vineyard. He put a wall around it, dug a pit for a winepress in it and built a watchtower. Then he rented the vineyard to some farmers and went away on a journey *for a long time.* When the harvest time approached, he sent *a servant* to the tenants to collect from them some of the fruit of the vineyard. The tenants seized his servant; beat him, and sent him away empty-handed. Then he sent another servant to them; they struck this man on the head and treated him shamefully. He sent still another, *a third, and they wounded him and threw him out.* He sent many others; some of them they beat, others they killed.

"*Then the owner of the vineyard said, 'What shall I do?'* He had one left to send. *'I will send my son, whom I love; perhaps they will respect him.'* But when the tenants saw the son, they *talked the matter over.* 'This is the heir. Come, let's kill him and take his inheritance.' So they took him and threw him out of the vineyard and killed him. Therefore, when the owner of the vineyard comes, what will he do to those tenants? 'He will bring those wretches to a wretched *end,' they* replied. *'Kill those tenants and give the vineyard to other tenants,* and he

---

Matthew   Mark   *Luke*   **John**

will share the crop at harvest time.' *When the people heard this, they said, 'May this never be!'"*

Jesus *looked directly at them and asked, "Then what is the meaning of that which is written* in the Scriptures, have you never read: 'The stone the builders rejected has become the capstone; the Lord has done this, and it is marvelous in our eyes?' Therefore, I tell you that the kingdom of God will be taken away from you and given to a people who will produce its fruit. He who falls on this stone will be broken to pieces, but he on whom it falls will be crushed." When the chief priests and the Pharisees heard Jesus' parables, they knew he *had spoken this parable against them.* They looked for a way to arrest him, but they were afraid of the crowd because the people held that he was a prophet.

Jesus spoke to them again in parables, saying: "The kingdom of heaven is like a king who prepared a wedding banquet for his son. He sent his servants to those who had been invited to the banquet to tell them to come, but they refused to come. Then he sent some more servants and said, 'Tell those who have been invited that I have prepared my dinner: my oxen and fattened cattle have been butchered, and everything is ready. Come to the wedding banquet.' But they paid no attention and went off—one to his field, another to his business. The rest seized his servants, mistreated them, and killed them. The king was enraged. He sent his army and destroyed those murderers and burned their city. Then he said to his servants, 'The wedding banquet is ready, but those I invited did not deserve to come. Go to the street corners and invite to the banquet anyone you find.' So the servants went out into the streets and gathered all the people they could find, both good and bad, and the wedding hall was filled with guests.

"But when the king came in to see the guests, he noticed a man there who was not wearing wedding clothes. 'Friend,' he asked, 'how did you get in here without wedding clothes?' The man was speechless. Then the king told the attendants, 'Tie him hand and foot

---

Matthew   Mark   *Luke*   **John**

15

and throw him outside into the darkness, where there will be weeping and gnashing of teeth.' For many are invited, but few are chosen."

The teachers of the law and the chief priests looked for a way to arrest him immediately because they knew he had spoken this parable against them. But they were afraid of the <u>crowd; so they left him and went away</u> <u>and</u> made plans to trap him.

Keeping a close watch on him, they sent spies who pretended to be honest. They hoped to catch Jesus in something he said so that they might hand him over to the power and authority of the governor. They sent their disciples to him along with the Herodians. "Teacher," they said, "we know you are a man of integrity and that you teach the way of God in accordance with the truth. You aren't swayed by men --- *you do not show partiality,* <u>but you teach the way of God in accordance</u> <u>with the truth.</u> Tell us then, what is your opinion? Is it right to pay taxes to Caesar or not? <u>Should we pay or shouldn't we?</u>" But Jesus, knowing <u>their hypocrisy</u>—their evil intent --- said, "You hypocrites, why are you trying to trap me? Show me <u>a denarius</u> - the coin used for paying the tax <u>and let me look at it.</u>" They brought him a denarius, and he asked them, "Whose portrait is this? And whose inscription?" "Caesar's," they replied. Then he said to them, "Give to Caesar what is Caesar's, and to God what is God's." When they heard this, they were amazed. *They were unable to trap him in what he had said there in public. And astonished by his answer, they became silent* and went away.

The same day the Sadducees, who say there is no resurrection, came to <u>Jesus</u> with a question. "Teacher," they said. "Moses *wrote for us that if a* man's brother dies *and leaves a wife but no children,* his brother must marry the widow and have children for *his brother.* Now there were seven brothers among us. The first one married *a woman* and died *childless* and, since he had no children, he left his wife to his brother. <u>The second one married the widow, but he also died leaving</u> <u>no child. It was the same with the third. In fact, none of the seven</u> <u>left any children. Last of all, the woman died too.</u> Now then, at the

---

resurrection, whose wife will she be of the seven, since all of them were married to her?"

Jesus replied, "<u>Are you not in error</u> because you do not know the Scriptures or the power of God? *The people of this age marry and are given in marriage. But those who are considered worthy of taking part in that age and in the resurrection from the dead will neither marry nor be given in marriage, and they can no longer die; for they are like the angels. They are God's children, since they are children of the resurrection.* But about the resurrection of the dead, have you not read <u>in the book of Moses, in the account of the bush,</u> what God said to you? *Even Moses showed that the dead rise, for he calls the Lord 'the God of Abraham, and the God of Isaac, and the God of Jacob.' He is not the God of the dead, but of the living, for to him all are alive.* <u>You are badly mistaken!</u>" When the crowds heard this, they were astonished at his teaching. *Some of the teachers of the law responded, "Well said, teacher!"*

Hearing that Jesus had silenced the Sadducees, the Pharisees got together. <u>One of the teachers of the law came</u>, an expert in the law, <u>and heard them debating</u>. <u>Noticing that Jesus had given them a good answer</u>, tested him with this question: "Teacher, which is the greatest commandment – *the most important one -* in the Law?" "<u>The most important one is this:</u> Jesus replied, '<u>Hear, O Israel</u>, love the Lord your God with all your heart and with all your soul and with all your mind <u>and with all your strength.</u>' This is the first and greatest commandment. And the second is like it: 'Love your neighbor as yourself.' <u>There is no commandment greater than these.</u> All the Law and the Prophets hang on these two commandments."

"<u>Well said, teacher,</u>" the man replied. "<u>You are right in saying that God is one and there is no other but him. To love him with all your heart, with all your understanding and with all your strength and to love your neighbor as yourself is more important than all burnt offerings and sacrifices.</u>" <u>When Jesus saw that he had answered wisely, he said to him, "You are not far from the kingdom of God."</u>

Matthew   <u>Mark</u>   *Luke*   **John**

While the Pharisees were gathered together <u>while Jesus was teaching in the temple courts,</u> Jesus asked them, "What do you think about the Christ? Whose son is he?" "The son of David," they replied. He said to them, "How is it then that David, speaking by the Spirit, *declares in the Book of Psalms: 'The Lord said to my Lord: sit at my right hand until I make your enemies a footstool for your feet.'* If then David calls him 'Lord,' how can he be his son?" No one could say a word in reply and, from that day on, no one dared to ask him any more questions.

<u>The large crowd listened to him with delight.</u> Then Jesus said to the crowds and to his disciples: "<u>Watch out for the teachers of the law.</u> The teachers of the law and the Pharisees sit in Moses' seat. So you must obey them and do everything they tell you. But do not do what they do, for they do not practice what they preach. They tie up heavy loads and put them on men's shoulders, but they themselves are not willing to lift a finger to move them. Everything they do is done for men to see: They make their phylacteries wide and the tassels on their garments long; they love the place of honor at banquets and the most important seats in the synagogues, *they devour widows' houses and for a show make lengthy prayers,* they love to be greeted in the marketplaces and to have men call them 'Rabbi.' *Such men will be punished most severely.*

"But you are not to be called 'Rabbi,' for you have only one Master and you are all brothers. And do not call anyone on earth 'father,' for you have one Father, and he is in heaven. Nor are you to be called 'teacher,' for you have one Teacher, the Christ. The greatest among you will be your servant. For whoever exalts himself will be humbled, and whoever humbles himself will be exalted.

"Woe to you, teachers of the law and Pharisees, you hypocrites! You shut the kingdom of heaven in men's faces. You yourselves do not enter, nor will you let those enter who are trying to. Woe to you, teachers of the law and Pharisees, you hypocrites! You travel over land

---

Matthew   <u>Mark</u>   *Luke*   **John**

and sea to win a single convert, and when he becomes one, you make him twice as much a son of hell as you are.

"Woe to you, blind guides! You say, 'If anyone swears by the temple, it means nothing; but if anyone swears by the gold of the temple, he is bound by his oath.' You blind fools! Which is greater: the gold or the temple that makes the gold sacred? You also say, 'If anyone swears by the altar, it means nothing; but if anyone swears by the gift on it, he is bound by his oath.' You blind men! Which is greater: the gift or the altar that makes the gift sacred? Therefore, he who swears by the altar swears by it and by everything on it. And he who swears by the temple swears by it and by the one who dwells in it. And he who swears by heaven swears by God's throne and by the one who sits on it.

"Woe to you, teachers of the law and Pharisees, you hypocrites! You give a tenth of your spices—mint, dill, and cumin. But you have neglected the more important matters of the law—justice, mercy, and faithfulness. You should have practiced the latter, without neglecting the former. You blind guides! You strain out a gnat but swallow a camel."

Jesus sat down opposite the place where the offerings were put and watched the crowd putting their money into the temple treasury but a poor widow came and put in two very small copper coins worth only a fraction of a penny. Calling his disciples to him, Jesus said, "I tell you the truth," he said, "this poor widow has put in more than all the others. All these people gave their gifts out of their wealth, but she out of her poverty put in all she had to live on.

"Woe to you, teachers of the law and Pharisees, you hypocrites! You clean the outside of the cup and dish, but inside they are full of greed and self-indulgence. Blind Pharisee! First clean the inside of the cup and dish, and then the outside also will be clean.

"Woe to you, teachers of the law and Pharisees, you hypocrites! You are like whitewashed tombs, which look beautiful on the outside

Matthew　　　　　　　Mark　　　　　　　*Luke*　　　　　　**John**

19

but on the inside are full of dead men's bones and everything unclean. In the same way, on the outside you appear to people as righteous, but on the inside you are full of hypocrisy and wickedness.

"Woe to you, teachers of the law and Pharisees, you hypocrites! You build tombs for the prophets and decorate the graves of the righteous. And you say, 'If we had lived in the days of our forefathers, we would not have taken part with them in shedding the blood of the prophets.' So you testify against yourselves that you are the descendants of those who murdered the prophets. Fill up, then, the measure of the sin of your forefathers! You snakes! You brood of vipers! How will you escape being condemned to hell?

"Therefore I am sending you prophets and wise men and teachers. Some of them you will kill and crucify; others you will flog in your synagogues and pursue from town to town. And so upon you will come all the righteous blood that has been shed on earth, from the blood of righteous Abel to the blood of Zechariah son of Berakiah, whom you murdered between the temple and the altar. I tell you the truth, all this will come upon this generation.

"O Jerusalem, Jerusalem, you who kill the prophets and stone those sent to you, how often I have longed to gather your children together, as a hen gathers her chicks under her wings, but you were not willing. Look, your house is left to you desolate. For I tell you, you will not see me again until you say, 'Blessed is he who comes in the name of the Lord.'"

Jesus left the temple and was walking away when *some of his disciples were remarking about how the temple was adorned with beautiful stones and with gifts dedicated to God.* "Look, Teacher! What massive stones! What magnificent buildings!" "Do you see all these great buildings?" he asked. *"As for what you see here, the time will come when not one stone will be left on another; every one of them will be thrown down."*

As Jesus was sitting on the Mount of Olives, Peter, James, John,

---

and Andrew came to him privately. "Tell us *teacher*," they said, "when will this happen, and what will be the sign of your coming and of the end of the age? <u>And what will be the sign that they are all about to be fulfilled?</u>" Jesus answered: "Watch out that no one deceives you. For many will come in my name claiming, 'I am the Christ' *and 'The time is near,'* and will deceive many. *Do not follow them.* You will hear of wars *and revolutions* and rumors of wars, but see to it that you are not alarmed. Such things must happen, but the end is still to come."

Then he said to them: "Nation will rise against nation and kingdom against kingdom. There will be famines and *great* earthquakes *and pestilences in various places and fearful events and great signs from heaven.* All these are the beginning of birth pains.

"<u>You must be on your guard</u>. Then you will be handed over <u>to the local councils and flogged in the synagogues</u> *and prisons* to be persecuted and put to death, and you will be hated by all nations because of me. <u>On account of me you will stand before governors and kings as witnesses to them</u> *and all on account of my name.* <u>And the gospel must first be preached to all nations. Whenever you are arrested and brought to trial, do not worry beforehand about what to say. Just say whatever is given you at the time, for it is not you speaking, but the Holy Spirit.</u> *For I will give you words and wisdom that none of your adversaries will be able to resist or contradict.* At that time many will turn away from the faith and will betray and hate each other, and many false prophets will appear and deceive many people. <u>Brother will betray brother to death and a father his child. Children will rebel against their parents and have them put to death. All men will hate you because of me.</u> *But not a hair of your head will perish.* Because of the increase of wickedness, the love of most will grow cold, but he who stands firm to the end will be saved. And this gospel of the kingdom will be preached in the whole world as a testimony to all nations, and then the end will come.

"*When you see Jerusalem surrounded by armies, you will know that*

Matthew   <u>Mark</u   *Luke*   **John**

21

its desolation is near. So when you see standing in the holy place 'the abomination that causes desolation,' spoken of through the prophet Daniel --- let the reader understand --- then let those who are in Judea flee to the mountains, *let those in the city get out, and let those in the country not enter the city.* Let no one on the roof of his house go down to take anything out of the house. Let no one in the field go back to get his cloak. *For this is the time of punishment in fulfillment of all that has been written.* How dreadful it will be in those days for pregnant women and nursing mothers! Pray that your flight will not take place in winter or on the Sabbath. For then there will be great distress, unequaled from the beginning of the world, <u>when God created the world</u>, until now—and never to be equaled again. *They will fall by the sword and will be taken as prisoners to all the nations. Jerusalem will be trampled on by the Gentiles until the times of the Gentiles are fulfilled.* If those days had not been cut short, no one would survive, but for the sake of the elect, <u>whom he has chosen</u>, those days will be shortened.

"*Watch out that you are not deceived.* At that time if anyone says to you, 'Look, here is the Christ!' or, 'Look, there he is!' do not believe it. For false Christs and false prophets will appear and perform great signs and miracles to deceive even the elect—if that were possible. <u>So be on your guard.</u> See, I have told you <u>everything</u> ahead of time. So if anyone tells you, 'There he is, out in the desert,' do not go out; or, 'Here he is, in the inner rooms,' do not believe it. For as the lightning comes from the east and flashes to the west, so will be the coming of the Son of Man. Wherever there is a carcass, there the vultures will gather.

"Immediately after the distress of those days the sun will be darkened, and the moon will not give its light; the stars will fall from the sky and the heavenly bodies will be shaken. *On the earth, nations will be in anguish and perplexity at the roaring and tossing of the sea. Men will faint in terror, apprehensive of what is coming on the world, for the heavenly bodies will be shaken'* At that time the sign of the Son

Matthew   <u>Mark</u>   *Luke*   **John**

of Man will appear in the sky, and all the nations of the earth will mourn. They will see the Son of Man coming on the clouds of the sky with power and great glory. And he will send his angels with a loud trumpet call, and they will gather his elect from the four winds, from <u>the ends of the earth to the ends of the heavens.</u> *When these things begin to take place, stand up and lift up your heads, because your redemption is drawing near."*

He told them this parable: "Look at the fig tree and all the trees. Now learn this lesson from the fig tree: as soon as its twigs get tender and its leaves come out – *when they sprout leaves --- you can see for yourselves and know* that summer is near. Even so, when you see all these things *happening,* you know that *the kingdom of God* is near, right at the door. I tell you the truth, this generation will certainly not pass away until all these things have happened. Heaven and earth will pass away, but my words will never pass away.

"No one knows about that day or hour, not even the angels in heaven, nor the Son, but only the Father. As it was in the days of Noah, so it will be at the coming of the Son of Man. For in the days before the flood, people were eating and drinking, marrying and giving in marriage, up to the day Noah entered the ark; and they knew nothing about what would happen until the flood came and took them all away. That is how it will be at the coming of the Son of Man. Two men will be in the field; one will be taken and the other left. Two women will be grinding with a hand mill; one will be taken and the other left.

"Be careful, or your hearts will be weighed down with dissipation, drunkenness, and the anxieties of life, and that day will close on you unexpectedly like a trap. For it will come upon all those who live on the face of the whole earth. Therefore, keep watch, <u>be on guard!</u> <u>Be alert!</u> You do not know on what day your Lord will come. <u>It's like a man going away: he leaves his house and puts his servants in charge, each with his assigned task, and tells the one at the door to keep watch.</u> But

understand this: if the owner of the house had known at what time of night the thief was coming, he would have kept watch and would not have let his house be broken into. So you also must be ready, because the Son of Man will come at an hour when you do not expect him – whether in the evening, or at midnight, or when the rooster crows, or at dawn. If he comes suddenly, do not let him find you sleeping. *Be always on the watch, and pray that you may be able to escape all that is about to happen and that you may be able to stand before the Son of Man.* What I say to you, I say to everyone: 'Watch!'

"Who then is the faithful and wise servant, whom the master has put in charge of the servants in his household to give them their food at the proper time? It will be good for that servant whose master finds him doing so when he returns. I tell you the truth, he will put him in charge of all his possessions. But suppose that servant is wicked and says to himself, 'My master is staying away a long time,' and he then begins to beat his fellow servants and to eat and drink with drunkards. The master of that servant will come on a day when he does not expect him and at an hour he is not aware of. He will cut him to pieces and assign him a place with the hypocrites, where there will be weeping and gnashing of teeth.

"At that time the kingdom of heaven will be like ten virgins who took their lamps and went out to meet the bridegroom. Five of them were foolish, and five were wise. The foolish ones took their lamps but did not take any oil with them. The wise, however, took oil in jars along with their lamps. The bridegroom was a long time in coming, and they all became drowsy and fell asleep. At midnight the cry rang out: 'Here's the bridegroom! Come out to meet him!' Then all the virgins woke up and trimmed their lamps. The foolish ones said to the wise, 'Give us some of your oil; our lamps are going out.'"

'No,' they replied, 'there may not be enough for both us and you. Instead, go to those who sell oil and buy some for yourselves.' But while they were on their way to buy the oil, the bridegroom arrived.

Matthew   <u>Mark</u>   *Luke*   **John**

The virgins who were ready went in with him to the wedding banquet. And the door was shut. Later the others also came. 'Sir! Sir!' they said. 'Open the door for us!' But he replied, 'I tell you the truth, I don't know you.' Therefore, keep watch, because you do not know the day or the hour.

"Again, it will be like a man going on a journey who called his servants and entrusted his property to them. To one he gave five talents of money, to another two talents, and to another one talent, each according to his ability. Then he went on his journey. The man who had received the five talents went at once and put his money to work and gained five more. So also, the one with the two talents gained two more. But the man who had received the one talent went off, dug a hole in the ground and hid his master's money.

"After a long time, the master of those servants returned and settled accounts with them. The man who had received the five talents brought the other five. 'Master,' he said, 'you entrusted me with five talents. See, I have gained five more.' His master replied, 'Well done, good and faithful servant! You have been faithful with a few things; I will put you in charge of many things. Come and share your master's happiness!'

"The man with the two talents also came. 'Master,' he said, 'you entrusted me with two talents; see, I have gained two more.' His master replied, 'Well done, good and faithful servant! You have been faithful with a few things; I will put you in charge of many things. Come and share your master's happiness!'

"Then the man who had received the one talent came. 'Master,' he said, "I knew that you are a hard man, harvesting where you have not sown and gathering where you have not scattered seed. So I was afraid and went out and hid your talent in the ground. See, here is what belongs to you.' His master replied, 'You wicked, lazy servant! So you knew that I harvest where I have not sown and gather where I have not scattered seed? Well then, you should have put my money on deposit with the bankers, so that when I returned I would have received it back with interest. Take the talent from him and give it to the one who has the ten talents. For everyone who has will be given more, and he will have an abundance. Whoever does not have, even what he has will be taken from him. And throw that worthless servant outside, into the darkness, where there will be weeping and gnashing of teeth.'

"When the Son of Man comes in his glory, and all the angels with him, he will sit on his throne in heavenly glory. All the nations will be gathered before him, and he will separate the people one from another as a shepherd separates the sheep from the goats. He will put the sheep on his right and the goats on his left. Then the King will say to those on his right, 'Come, you who are blessed by my Father; take your inheritance, the kingdom prepared for you since the creation of the world. For I was hungry and you gave me something to eat, I was thirsty and you gave me something to drink, I was a stranger and you invited me in, I needed clothes and you clothed me, I was sick and you looked after me, I was in prison and you came to visit me.'

"Then the righteous will answer him, 'Lord, when did we see you hungry and feed you or thirsty and give you something to drink? When did we see you a stranger and invite you in or needing clothes and clothe you? When did we see you sick or in prison and go to visit you?' The King will reply, 'I tell you the truth, whatever you did for one of the least of these brothers of mine, you did for me.'

"Then he will say to those on his left, 'Depart from me, you who are cursed, into the eternal fire prepared for the devil and his angels. For I was hungry, and you gave me nothing to eat, I was thirsty and you gave me nothing to drink, I was a stranger and you did not invite me in, I needed clothes and you did not clothe me, I was sick and in prison and you did not look after me.'

"They also will answer, 'Lord, when did we see you hungry or thirsty or a stranger or needing clothes or sick or in prison, and did not help you?' He will reply, 'I tell you the truth, whatever you did not do for one of the least of these, you did not do for me.' Then they will go away to eternal punishment, but the righteous to eternal life."

Each day Jesus was teaching at the temple, and each evening he went out to spend the night on the hill called the Mount of Olives, and all the people, the chief priests, and the elders of the people *came early in the morning to hear him at the temple.*

When Jesus had finished saying all these things, he said to his disciples, "As you know, the Passover, the Feast of Unleavened Bread, is two days away and the Son of Man will be handed over to be crucified." Then the chief priests and the elders of the people and the teachers of the law assembled in the palace of the high priest, whose name was Caiaphas, and were looking for some sly way to arrest Jesus and kill him. "But not during the Feast," they said, "or there may be a riot among the people" *because they were afraid of the people.*

Tues/Wednesday

(Matthew 26:6-16; Mark 14:3-11;
Luke 22:11-13; John 12:20-50 [NIV])

13th of Nisan:

*The disciples asked Jesus where he wanted them to make preparation to eat the Passover meal. The word used in the Greek for the official preparation day is **paraskeue**, but the word used by Matthew, Mark, and Luke is **hetoimazo**, which is the word for **getting ready**. The Jewish people, then and today, take a day to remove the leaven from everything in the house. This takes time.*

Why didn't Jesus just tell the disciples where to go to make preparations? Possibly He didn't want Judas to know where the supper would be held until later because Judas was looking for an opportunity to have Him arrested. Jesus didn't want to be arrested yet, because He had to die on Thursday, the 14th, to fulfill every aspect of being our Passover lamb.

___

While Jesus was in Bethany, reclining at the table in the home of a man known as Simon the Leper, a woman came with an alabaster jar of very expensive perfume, made of pure nard. She broke the jar and poured the perfume on his head as he was reclining at the table. Some of those present were saying indignantly to one another, "Why this waste of perfume? It could have been sold for more than a year's wages and the money given to the poor." And they rebuked her harshly.

Aware of this, Jesus said, "Leave her alone. Why are you bothering her? She has done a beautiful thing to me. The poor you will always have with you, and you can help them any time you want. But you

Matthew   Mark   Luke   John

will not always have me. She did what she could. She poured perfume on my body beforehand to prepare for my burial. I tell you the truth, whenever the gospel is preached throughout the world, what she has done will also be told, in memory of her."

(It is uncertain on which day this event happened. I placed it here.) **Now there were some Greeks among those who went up to worship at the Feast. They came to Philip, who was from Bethsaida in Galilee, with a request. "Sir," they said, "we would like to see Jesus." Philip went to tell Andrew; Andrew and Philip in turn told Jesus. Jesus replied, "The hour has come for the Son of Man to be glorified. I tell you the truth, unless a kernel of wheat falls to the ground and dies, it remains only a single seed. But if it dies, it produces many seeds. The man who loves his life will lose it, while the man who hates his life in this world will keep it for eternal life. Whoever serves me must follow me; and where I am, my servant also will be. My Father will honor the one who serves me. Now my heart is troubled, and what shall I say? 'Father, save me from this hour'? No, it was for this very reason I came to this hour. Father glorify your name!" Then a voice came from heaven, "I have glorified it, and will glorify it again. The crowd that was there and heard it said it had thundered; others said an angel had spoken to him."**

Jesus said, "This voice was for your benefit, not mine. Now is the time for judgment on this world; now the prince of this world will be driven out. But I, when I am lifted up from the earth, will draw all men to myself." He said this to show the kind of death he was going to die.

The crowd spoke up, "We have heard from the Law that the Christ will remain forever, so how can you say, 'The Son of Man must be lifted up?' Then Jesus told them, "You are going to have the light just a little while longer. Walk while you have the light, before darkness overtakes you. The man who walks in the dark does not know where he is going. Put your trust in the light while you have it, so that you may become sons of light." When he had finished speaking, Jesus left and hid himself from them.

Even after Jesus had done all these miraculous signs in their presence, they still would not believe in him. This was to fulfill the word of Isaiah the prophet: "Lord, who has believed our message and to whom has the arm of the Lord been revealed?" For this reason they could not believe, because, as Isaiah says elsewhere: "He has blinded their eyes and deadened their hearts, so they can neither see with their eyes, nor understand with their hearts, nor turn – and I would heal them."

Isaiah said this because he saw Jesus' glory and spoke about him. Yet at the same time many even among the leaders believed in him. But because of the Pharisees they would not confess their faith for fear they would be put out of the synagogue; for they loved praise from men more than praise from God.

Then Jesus cried out, "When a man believes in me, he does not believe in me only, but in the one who sent me. When he looks at me, he sees the one who sent me. I have come into the world as a light, so that no one who believes in me should stay in darkness. As for the person who hears my words but does not keep them, I do not judge him. For I did not come to judge the world, but to save it. There is a judge for the one who rejects me and does not accept my words; that very word which I spoke will condemn him at the last day. For I did not speak of my own accord, but the Father who sent me commanded me what to say and how to say it. I know that his command leads to eternal life. So whatever I say is just what the Father has told me to say."

Now the Feast of Unleavened Bread, called the Passover, was approaching, and the chief priests and the teachers of the law were looking for some way to get rid of Jesus, for they were afraid of the people. Then Satan entered Judas, one of the Twelve. The one called Judas Iscariot

| Matthew | Mark | *Luke* | John |

went to the chief priests *and officers of the temple guard and discussed with them how he might betray Jesus* and asked, "What are you willing to give me if I hand him over to you?" <u>They were delighted to hear this and promised to give him money.</u> *He consented,* so they counted out for him thirty silver coins. From then on Judas watched for an opportunity to hand him over to them *when no crowd was present.*

On the first day of the Feast of Unleavened Bread, <u>when it was customary to sacrifice the Passover lamb</u>, the disciples came to Jesus and asked, "Where do you want us to make preparations for you to eat the Passover?" <u>So he sent two of his disciples,</u> *Peter and John,* <u>telling them,</u> *"Go and make preparations for us to eat the Passover,"*

He replied, "Go into the city – *as you enter,* <u>a man carrying a jar of water will meet you. Follow him</u> *to the house that he enters.* <u>Say to the owner of the house he enters,</u> 'The Teacher says: My appointed time is near. I am going to celebrate the Passover with my disciples at your house. <u>Where is my guest room where I may eat the Passover with my disciples?'</u> <u>He will show you a large upper room, furnished and ready.</u> <u>Make preparations for us there."</u>

So the disciples did as Jesus had directed them; <u>went into the city and found things just as Jesus had told them</u> and did as Jesus had directed them and prepared the Passover.

Wed/Thursday

(Matthew 26:17-27:61; Mark 14:12-15:47;
Luke 22:14-23:56, **John 13:1-19:42** [NIV])

14th of Nisan:

In Luke 22:15 & 16, we read:

> And he said unto them, "I have eagerly desired to eat
> this Passover with you before I suffer. For I tell you, I will
> not eat it again until it finds fulfillment in the kingdom
> of God." (NIV)

The word **for** connecting the two halves of the statement is **gar**, a particle used for assigning a reason or explanation. So it could be translated **but, as,** or **because**. Thus, the words **lego gar humin** could be translated **But I must inform you,** so the verse would read:

> And he said unto them, "I have eagerly desired to eat
> this Passover with you before I suffer; but I must inform
> you I will not eat it again until it finds fulfillment in the
> kingdom of God."

On the evening of the 14th, Wednesday night, the disciples and Jesus go to Jerusalem for the last supper. Nowhere does the Bible call this meal anything other than a regular meal. There is no mention of a Passover lamb being sacrificed or eaten. The meal is called a **supper.** However, wonderful things happened at that supper:

1. Jesus washes their feet;
2. The Lord's Supper is instituted, and

Matthew   Mark   Luke   John

3. Jesus' farewell message is given to His disciples.

Hebrews 10: 1, 3, 4, 9, 10 & 14 say:

> *The law is only a shadow of the good things that are coming .... For this reason it can never, by the same sacrifices repeated endlessly year after year, make perfect those who draw near to worship. ...But those sacrifices are an annual reminder of sins because it is impossible for the blood of bulls and goats to take away sins. ... Then he said, "Here I am, I have come to do your will." He sets aside the first to establish the second. And by that will, we have been made holy through the sacrifice of the body of Jesus Christ once for all. ...For by one sacrifice he has made perfect forever those who are being made holy." (NIV)"*

The annual sacrifice for sin that the Jewish people offered was looking forward to the sacrifice of Jesus shedding His sinless blood on the cross to pay for our sin.

When Jesus was crucified, He was placed between two criminals – sinners. One of them believed Jesus was the Christ and was saved, but the other did not. Still today, Jesus is the divider of mankind. Those who accept and believe in Him are saved, cleansed from their sins, and spend eternity with Him in heaven.

Notice that Jesus gets no rest this night. He is up all night. First He talks late into the night teaching the disciples --- then He is up the rest of the night appearing before Annas and then Caiaphas before being taken to the Roman governor.

Matthew   <u>Mark</u   *Luke*   **John**

35

When the hour came, Jesus and his disciples reclined at the table. **It was just before the Passover Feast. Jesus knew that the time had come for him to leave this world and go to the Father. Jesus knew that the Father had put all things under his power, and that he had come from God and was returning to God.** *And he said to them, "I have eagerly desired to eat this Passover with you before I suffer. For I tell you, I will not eat it again until it finds fulfillment in the kingdom of God."*

Also a dispute arose among them as to which of them was considered to be greatest. Jesus said to them, "The kings of the Gentiles lord it over them, and those who exercise authority over them call themselves Benefactors. But you are not to be like that. Instead, the greatest among you should be like the youngest, and the one who rules like the one who serves. For who is greater, the one who is at the table or the one who serves? Is it not the one who is at the table? But I am among you as one who serves. You are those who have stood by me in my trials. And I confer on you a kingdom, just as my Father conferred one on me, so that you may eat and drink at my table in my kingdom and sit on thrones, judging the twelve tribes of Israel."

Having loved his own who were in the world, he now showed them the full extent of his love. The evening meal was being served, and the devil had already prompted Judas Iscariot, son of Simon, to betray Jesus. Jesus knew that the Father had put all things under his power and that he had come from God and was returning to God; so he got up from the meal, took off his outer clothing and wrapped a towel around his waist. After that, he poured water into a basin and began to wash his disciples' feet, drying them with the towel that was wrapped around him.

He came to Simon Peter who said to him, "Lord, are you going to wash my feet?" Jesus replied, "You do not realize now what I am doing, but later you will understand." "No," said Peter, "you shall never wash my feet." Jesus answered, "Unless I wash you, you have no part with me." "Then, Lord," Simon Peter replied, "not just my feet but my hands and my head as well!" Jesus answered, "A person

---

Matthew   <u>Mark</u>   *Luke*   **John**

who has had a bath needs only to wash his feet; his whole body is clean. And you are clean, though not every one of you." For he knew who was going to betray him, and that was why he said not everyone was clean.

When he finished washing their feet, he put on his clothes and returned to his place. "Do you understand what I have done for you?" he asked them. "You call me 'Teacher' and 'Lord,' and rightly so, for that is what I am. Now that I, your Lord and Teacher, have washed your feet, you also should wash one another's feet. I have set you an example that you should do as I have done for you. I tell you the truth, no servant is greater than his master nor is a messenger greater than the one who sent him. Now that you know these things, you will be blessed if you do them.

"I am not referring to all of you; I know those I have chosen. But this is to fulfill the scriptures: 'He who shares my bread has lifted up his heel against me.' I am telling you now before it happens so that when it does happen you will believe that I am He. I tell you the truth, whoever accepts anyone I send accepts me; and whoever accepts me accepts the one who sent me."

After he had said this, while they were reclining at the table eating, Jesus was troubled in spirit and testified, "I tell you the truth, one of you is going to betray me." His disciples stared at one another, at a loss to know which of them he meant. They were very sad and began to say to him one after the other, "Surely not I, Lord?" One of them, the disciple whom Jesus loved, was reclining next to him. Simon Peter motioned to this disciple and said, "Ask him which one he means." Leaning back against Jesus, he asked him, "Lord, who is it?" Jesus answered, "It is the one who is eating with me – one of the Twelve, the one to whom I will give this piece of bread when I have dipped it in the dish." Then, dipping the piece of bread, he gave it to Judas Iscariot, son of Simon. As soon as Judas took the bread, Satan entered into him. The Son of Man will go just

---

as it is written about him. But woe to that man who betrays the Son of Man! It would be better for him if he had not been born." Then Judas, the one who would betray him, said "Surely not I, Rabbi?" Jesus answered, "Yes, it is you. **What you are about to do, do quickly,"** Jesus told him, but no one at the meal understood why Jesus said this to him. Since Judas had charge of the money, some thought Jesus was telling him to buy what was needed for the Feast, or to give something to the poor. As soon as Judas had taken the bread, he went out. And it was night.

When he was gone, Jesus said, "Now is the Son of Man glorified and God is glorified in him. If God is glorified in him, God will glorify the Son in himself, and will glorify him at once."

While they were eating, Jesus took bread, gave thanks and broke it, and gave it to his disciples, saying, "Take and eat; this is my body *given for you; do this in remembrance of me."* Then *in the same way after the supper,* he took the cup, gave thanks and offered it to them, saying, "Drink from it, all of you. This is my blood of the *new* covenant which is poured out for many for the forgiveness of sins. I tell you, I will not drink of this fruit of the vine from now on until that day when I drink it anew with you in my Father's kingdom."

Then Jesus told them, "This very night you will all fall away on account of me, for it is written: 'I will strike the shepherd, and the sheep of the flock will be scattered.' But after I have risen, I will go ahead of you into Galilee. **My children, I will be with you only a little longer. You will look for me, and just as I told the Jews, so I tell you now: Where I am going, you cannot come. A new command I give you: Love one another as I have loved you, so you must love one another. All men will know that you are my disciples if you love one another."** Simon Peter said, "Lord, where are you going?" Jesus replied, "Where I am going, you cannot follow now, but you will follow later."

Peter asked, "Lord, why can't I follow you now? I will lay down my life for you." Then Jesus answered, "Will you really lay down your life for me? *Simon, Simon, Satan has asked to sift you as wheat. But I have prayed for you, Simon, that your faith may not fail. And when you have turned back, strengthen your brothers.*" Peter replied, "Even if all fall away on account of you, I never will, *I am ready to go with you to prison and to death.*" "I tell you the truth." Jesus answered, "<u>today</u> – <u>yes, tonight</u> – before the rooster crows <u>twice</u>, you <u>yourself</u> will disown me three times, *you will deny three times that you know me.*" But Peter <u>insisted emphatically,</u> "Even if I have to die with you, I will never disown you." And all the other disciples said the same.

Then Jesus asked them, *"When I sent you without purse, bag, or sandals, did you lack anything?" "Nothing," they answered." He said to them, "But now if you have a purse, take it, and also a bag; and if you don't have a sword, sell you cloak and buy one. It is written, 'And he was numbered with the transgressors,' and I tell you that this must be fulfilled in me. Yes, what is written about me is reaching its fulfillment." The disciples said, "See, Lord, here are two swords." "That's enough!" he replied.*

"Do not let your hearts be troubled. Trust in God, trust also in me. In my Father's house are many rooms; if it were not so, I would have told you. I am going there to prepare a place for you. And if I go and prepare a place for you, I will come back and take you to be with me that you also may be where I am. You know the way to the place where I am going." Thomas said to him, "Lord, we don't know where you are going, so how can we know the way?" Jesus answered, "I am the way and the truth and the life. No one comes to the Father except through me. If you really knew me, you would know my Father as well. From now on, you do know him and have seen him."

Philip said, "Lord, show us the Father and that will be enough for us." Jesus answered: "Don't you know me Philip, even after I have been among you such a long time? Anyone who has seen me has seen the Father. How can you say, 'Show us the Father'? Don't you believe that I am in the Father and that the Father is in me? The words I say to you are not just my own. Rather, it is the Father living in me who is doing his work. Believe me when I say that I am in the Father and that the Father is in me; or at least believe on the evidence of the miracles themselves. I tell you the truth, anyone who has faith in me will do what I have been doing. He will do even greater things than these, because I am going to the Father. And I will do whatever you ask in my name so that the Son may bring glory to the Father. You may ask me for anything in my name, and I will do it.

"If you love me, you will obey what I command. And I will ask the Father, and he will give you another Counselor to be with you forever – the Spirit of truth. The world cannot accept him because it neither sees him nor knows him. But you know him, for he lives with you and will be in you. I will not leave you as orphans; I will come to you. Before long, the world will not see me anymore, but you will see me. Because I live, you also will live. On that day you will realize that I am in my Father, and you are in me, and I am in you. Whoever has my commands and obeys them, he is the one who loves me. He who loves me will be loved by my Father, and I too will love him and show myself to him."

Then Judas (not Judas Iscariot) said, "But Lord, why do you intend to show yourself to us and not to the world?" Jesus replied, "If anyone loves me, he will obey my teaching. My Father will love him, and we will come to him and make our home with him. He who does not love me will not obey my teaching. These words you hear are not my own, they belong to the Father who sent me.

"All this I have spoken while still with you. But the Counselor, the Holy Spirit, whom the Father will send in my name, will teach you all things and will remind you of everything I have said to you. Peace I leave with you; my peace I give you. I do not give to you as the world gives. Do not let your hearts be troubled and do not be afraid.

"You heard me say, 'I am going away and I am coming back to you.' If you loved me, you would be glad that I am going to the Father, for the Father is greater than I. I have told you now before it happens, so that when it does happen you will believe. I will not speak with you much longer, for the prince of this world is coming. He has no hold on me, but the world must learn that I love the Father and that I do exactly what my Father has commanded me.

"Come now; let us leave." When they had sung a hymn *Jesus went out to the Mount of Olives, and his disciples followed him.*

"I am the vine, and my Father is the gardener. He cuts off every branch in me that bears no fruit, while every branch that does bear fruit he prunes so that it will be even more fruitful. You are already clean because of the word I have spoken to you. Remain in me, and I will remain in you. No branch can bear fruit by itself; it must remain in the vine. Neither can you bear fruit unless you remain in me.

"I am the vine, you are the branches. If a man remains in me and I in him, he will bear much fruit; apart from me you can do nothing. If anyone does not remain in me, he is like a branch that is thrown away and withers; such branches are picked up, thrown into the fire and burned. If you remain in me and my words remain in you, ask whatever you wish, and it will be given you. This is to my Father's glory that you bear fruit, showing yourselves to be my disciples.

"As the Father has loved me, so have I loved you. Now remain in my love. If you obey my commands, you will remain in my love, just as I have obeyed my Father's commands and remain in his love. I have told you this so that my joy may be in you and that your joy may be complete. My command is this: Love each other as I have loved you. Greater love has no one than this, that he lay

---

down his life for his friends. You are my friends if you do what I command. I no longer call you servants, because a servant does not know his master's business. Instead, I have called you friends, for everything that I learned from my Father I have made known to you. You did not choose me, but I chose you to go and bear fruit – fruit that will last. Then the Father will give you whatever you ask in my name. This is my command: Love each other.

"If the world hates you, keep in mind that it hated me first. If you belonged to the world, it would love you as its own. As it is, you do not belong to the world, but I have chosen you out of the world. That is why the world hates you. Remember the words I spoke to you: 'No servant is greater than his master.' If they persecuted me, they will persecute you also. If they obeyed my teaching, they will obey yours also. They will treat you this way because of my name, for they do not know the One who sent me. If I had not come and spoken to them, they would not be guilty of sin. Now, however, they have no excuse for their sin. He who hates me hates my Father as well. If I had not done among them what no one else did, they would not be guilty of sin. But now they have seen these miracles, and yet they have hated both me and my Father. But this is to fulfill what is written in their Law: 'They hated me without reason.'

"When the counselor comes, whom I will send to you from the Father, the Spirit of truth who goes out from the Father, he will testify about me, but you also must testify, for you have been with me from the beginning.

"All this I have told you so that you will not go astray. They will put you out of the synagogue, in fact, a time is coming when anyone who kills you will think he is offering a service to God. They will do such things because they have not known the Father or me. I have told you this so that when the time comes you will remember that I warned you. I did not tell you this at first because I was with you.

Matthew   Mark   *Luke*   **John**

"Now I am going to him who sent me, yet none of you asks me, "Where are you going?" Because I have said these things, you are filled with grief. But I tell you the truth: It is for your good that I am going away. Unless I go away, the Counselor will not come to you; but if I go, I will send him to you. When he comes, he will convict the world of guilt in regard to sin and righteousness and judgment; in regard to sin, because men do not believe in me; in regard to righteousness, because I am going to the Father where you can see me no longer; and in regard to judgment because the prince of this world now stands condemned.

"I have much more to say to you, more than you can now bear. But when he, the Spirit of truth, comes he will guide you into all truth. He will not speak on his own; he will speak only what he hears, and he will tell you what is yet to come. He will bring glory to me by taking from what is mine and making it known to you. All that belongs to the Father is mine. That is why I said the Spirit will take from what is mine and make it known to you. In a little while you will see me no more, and then after a little while you will see me."

Some of his disciples said to one another, "What does he mean by saying, 'In a little while you will see me no more, and then after a little while you will see me,' and 'Because I am going to the Father'?" They kept asking, "What does he mean by 'a little while'? We don't understand what he is saying."

Jesus saw that they wanted to ask him about this, so he said to them, "Are you asking one another what I meant when I said, 'In a little while you will see me no more and then after a little while you will see me'? I tell you the truth, you will weep and mourn while the world rejoices. You will grieve, but your grief will turn to joy. A woman giving birth to a child has pain because her time has come; but when her baby is born she forgets the anguish because of her joy that a child is born into the world. So with you: Now is your

Matthew   Mark   Luke   John

time of grief, but I will see you again, and you will rejoice and no one will take away your joy. In that day you will no longer ask me anything. I tell you the truth, my Father will give you whatever you ask in my name. Until now you have not asked for anything in my name. Ask and you will receive, and your joy will be complete.

"Though I have been speaking figuratively, a time is coming when I will no longer use this kind of language but will tell you plainly about my Father. In that day you will ask in my name. I am not saying that I will ask the Father on your behalf. No, the Father himself loves you because you have loved me and have believed that I came from God. I came from the Father and entered the world; now I am leaving the world and going back to the Father."

Then the disciples said, "Now you are speaking clearly and without figures of speech. Now we can see that you know all things and that you do not even need to have anyone ask you questions. This makes us believe that you came from God."

"You believe at last!" Jesus answered. "But a time is coming and has come when you will be scattered, each to his own home. You will leave me all alone. Yet I am not alone for my Father is with me. I have told you these things so that in me you may have peace. In this world you will have trouble. But take heart! I have overcome the world."

After Jesus said this, he looked toward heaven and prayed: "Father, the time has come. Glorify your Son that your Son may glorify you. For you granted him authority over all people that he might give eternal life to all those you have given him. Now this is eternal life: that they may know you, the only true God, and Jesus Christ, whom you have sent. I have brought you glory on earth by completing the work you gave me to do. And now, Father, glorify me in your presence with the glory I had with you before the world began.

"I have revealed you to those whom you gave me out of the

Matthew   Mark   *Luke*   **John**

44

world. They were yours; you gave them to me, and they have obeyed your word. Now they know that everything you have given me comes from you. For I gave them the words you gave me, and they accepted them. They knew with certainty that I came from you, and they believed that you sent me. I pray for them. I am not praying for the world, but for those you have given me, for they are yours. All I have is yours, and all you have is mine. And glory has come to me through them. I will remain in the world no longer, but they are still in the world, and I am coming to you. Holy Father, protect them by the power of your name – the name you gave me – so that they may be one as we are one! While I was with them, I protected them and kept them safe by that name you gave me. None has been lost except the one doomed to destruction so that Scripture would be fulfilled.

"I am coming to you now, but I say these things while I am still in the world so that they may have the full measure of my joy within them. I have given them your word and the world has hated them, for they are not of the world any more than I am of the world. My prayer is not that you take them out of the world but that you protect them from the evil one. They are not of the world, even as I am not of it. Sanctify them by the truth; your word is truth. As you sent me into the world, I have sent them into the world. For them I sanctify myself that they too may be truly sanctified.

"My prayer is not for them alone. I pray also for those who will believe in me through their message that all of them may be one, Father, just as you are in me and I am in you. May they also be in us so that the world may believe that you have sent me. I have given them the glory that you gave me that they may be one as we are one: I in them and you in me. May they be brought to complete unity to let the world know that you sent me and have loved them even as you have loved me.

Matthew   <u>Mark</u>   *Luke*   John

"Father, I want those you have given me to be with me where I am and to see my glory, the glory you have given me because you loved me before the creation of the world. Righteous Father, though the world does not know you, I know you, and they know that you have sent me. I have made you known to them and will continue to make you known in order that the love you have for me may be in them and that I myself may be in them."

When he had finished praying, Jesus left with his disciples and crossed the Kidron Valley. On the other side there was an olive grove, and he and his disciples went into it – Jesus went with his disciples to a place called Gethsemane. *On reaching the place,* <u>Jesus said to his disciples,</u> "Sit here while I go over there and pray." He took Peter and the two sons of Zebedee, <u>James and John,</u> along with him, and he began to be <u>deeply distressed</u>, sorrowful, and troubled. Then he said to them, "My soul is overwhelmed with sorrow to the point of death. Stay here and keep watch with me. *Pray that you will not fall into temptation.*" *He withdrew about a stone's throw beyond them.* He fell with his face to the ground and prayed, <u>"Abba, Father, he said, everything is possible for you. Take this cup from me.</u> Yet not as I will, but as you will."

Then he returned to his disciples and found them sleeping. <u>"Simon,"</u> he said to Peter, <u>"are you asleep? Could you not keep watch for one hour?</u> Watch and pray so that you will not fall into temptation. The spirit is willing, but the body is weak."

He went away a second time, *knelt down and prayed, "My Father, if you are willing, take this cup from me; if it is not possible for this cup to be taken away unless I drink it, may your will be done." An angel from heaven appeared to him and strengthened him. And being in anguish, he prayed more earnestly and his sweat was like drops of blood falling to the ground. When he rose from prayer and went back to the disciples,* he again found them sleeping, because their eyes were heavy. <u>They did not know what to say to him.</u> So he left them and went away once more and prayed the third time, saying the same thing.

Matthew   <u>Mark</u   *Luke*   **John**

Then he returned to the disciples and said to them, "Are you still sleeping and resting? Look, the hour is near, and the Son of Man is betrayed into the hands of sinners. Rise! Let us go! Here comes my betrayer!" **Now Judas, who betrayed him, knew the place because Jesus had often met there with his disciples. While he was still speaking, a crowd came up and the man who was called Judas, one of the Twelve, guiding a detachment of soldiers and some officials from the chief priests and Pharisees. They were carrying torches, lanterns, and weapons.**

Now the betrayer had arranged a signal with them. "The one I kiss is the man; arrest him <u>and lead him away under guard</u>." Going at once to Jesus, Judas said, "Greetings, Rabbi." He approached Jesus to kiss him, but Jesus asked him, "Judas, are you betraying the Son of *Man with a kiss?"* Jesus replied, "Friend, do what you came for." **Jesus, knowing all that was going to happen to him, went out and asked them, "Who is it you want?" "Jesus of Nazareth," they replied. "I am he," Jesus said. (And Judas the traitor was standing there with them.) When Jesus said, "I am he," they drew back and fell to the ground.**

Again he asked them, "Who is it you want?" And they said, "Jesus of Nazareth." "I told you that I am he," Jesus answered. "If you are looking for me, then let these men go." This happened so that the words he had spoken would be fulfilled: "I have not lost one of those you gave me." *When Jesus' followers saw what was going to happen, they said, "Lord, should we strike with our swords?"* With that, one of Jesus' companions, **Simon Peter, who had a sword,** reached for his sword, **drew it out, and struck the high priest's servant,** cutting off his **right ear. (The servant's name was Malchus.) Jesus commanded Peter,** "Put your sword back in its place, for all who draw the sword will die by the sword. Do you think I cannot call on my Father and he will at once put at my disposal more than twelve legions of angels? But how then would the Scriptures be fulfilled that

---

say it must happen this way?" *And he touched the man's ear and healed him.* "**Shall I not drink the cup the Father has given me?**"

At that time Jesus said to the crowds, <u>chief priests, the officers of the temple guard, and the elders who had come for him,</u> "Am I leading a rebellion that you have come out with swords and clubs to capture me? Every day <u>I was with you;</u> I sat in the temple courts teaching, and you did not arrest me. But this has all taken place that the writings of the prophets might be fulfilled. *But this is your hour – when darkness reigns."* Then all the disciples deserted him and fled. <u>A young man, wearing nothing but a linen garment, was following Jesus. When they seized him, he fled naked, leaving his garment behind.</u>

Then the detachment of soldiers with its commander and the Jewish officials arrested Jesus. They bound him and brought him first to Annas who was the father-in-law of Caiaphas, the high priest that year. Caiaphas was the one who had advised the Jews that it would be good if one man died for the people. Meanwhile, the high priest questioned Jesus about his disciples and his teaching. "I have spoken openly to the world," Jesus replied. "I always taught in synagogues or at the temple, where all the Jews come together. I said nothing in secret. Why question me? Ask those who heard me. Surely they know what I said." When Jesus said this, one of the officials nearby struck him in the face. "Is that any way to answer the high priest?" he demanded. "If I said something wrong," Jesus replied, "testify as to what is wrong. But if I spoke the truth, why did you strike me?" Then Annas sent him, still bound, to Caiaphas the high priest, where the teachers of the law and the elders had assembled.

***

But Peter **and another disciple** followed him at a distance. **Because this other disciple was known to the high priest, he**

Matthew   <u>Mark</u   *Luke*   **John**

48

went with Jesus into the high priest's courtyard, but Peter had to wait outside at the door. The other disciple, who was known to the high priest, came back, spoke to the girl on duty there, and brought Peter in. It was cold, and the servants and officials had kindled a fire they had made to keep warm *in the middle of the courtyard and had sat down together.* **Peter was standing there with them, warming himself.** While Peter was below in the courtyard, one of the servant girls of the high priest *saw him seated there in the firelight* and came by. When she saw Peter warming himself, she looked closely at him *and said,* "You also were with that Nazarene, Jesus," she said. But he denied it before them all. "*Woman,* I don't know or understand what you're talking about," he said and went out into the entryway.

***

The chief priests and the whole Sanhedrin were looking for false evidence against Jesus so that they could put him to death. But they did not find any, though many false witnesses came forward, but their statements did not agree. Finally two came forward and declared, "We heard him say, 'I am able to destroy this man-made temple of God and in three days build another, not made by man.'" Yet even then their testimony did not agree. Then the high priest stood up and said to Jesus, "Are you not going to answer? What is this testimony that these men are bringing against you?" But Jesus remained silent and gave no answer. Again the high priest said to him, "I charge you under oath by the living God: tell us if you are the Christ, the Son of God." "Yes, it is as you say," Jesus replied. "But I say to all of you: in the future you will see the Son of Man sitting at the right hand of the Mighty One and coming on the clouds of heaven."

Matthew   Mark   *Luke*   **John**

***

A little later, someone else <u>saw him (Peter) there</u>. <u>She said again to those standing around.</u> "<u>This fellow is one of them.</u>" <u>Again he denied it</u> with an oath, "I don't know the man!"

***

Then the high priest tore his clothes and said, "He has spoken blasphemy! Why do we need any more witnesses? Look, now you have heard the blasphemy. What do you think?" "He is worthy of death," they <u>all</u> answered. Then <u>some</u> spit in his face. *The men who were guarding Jesus began mocking and beating him,* <u>they blindfolded him,</u> and struck him with their fists. Others slapped him and said, "Prophesy to us, Christ. Who hit you?" <u>And the guards took him and beat him.</u> *And they said many other insulting things to him.*

***

<u>*After a little while, those standing near said to Peter,*</u> "*Surely you are one of them, for you are a Galilean, your accent gives you away.*" <u>*He began to call down curses on himself and he swore to them, "I don't know this man you're talking about."*</u> <u>*Immediately*</u> *just as he was speaking,* <u>*the rooster crowed the second time.*</u> *The Lord turned and looked straight at Peter.* <u>*Then Peter remembered the word Jesus had spoken to him.*</u> "<u>*Before the rooster crows twice you will disown me three times.*</u>" <u>*And he*</u> *went outside,* <u>*broke down, and wept*</u> *bitterly.*

***

At daybreak, <u>very early in the morning</u>, all the chief priests, <u>with the elders, the teachers of the law and the whole Sanhedrin,</u>

met together, and Jesus was led before them. "If you are the Christ," they *said, "tell us." Jesus answered, "If I tell you, you will not believe me, and* *if I asked you, you would not answer. But from now on, the Son of Man* *will be seated at the right hand of the mighty God." They all answered,* *"Are you then the Son of God?" He replied, "You are right in saying I* *am." Then they said, "Why do we need any more testimony? We have* *heard it from his own lips." They* <u>reached a decision</u> to put Jesus to death. *Then the whole assembly rose,* bound him, led him away **to the palace of the Roman governor,** and handed him over to Pilate, the governor.

***

When Judas, who had betrayed him, saw that Jesus was condemned, he was seized with remorse and returned the thirty silver coins to the chief priests and the elders. "I have sinned" he said; "for I have betrayed innocent blood." "What is that to us?" they replied. "That's your responsibility." So Judas threw the money into the temple and left. Then he went away and hanged himself.

The chief priests picked up the coins and said, "It is against the law to put this into the treasury, since it is blood money." So they decided to use the money to buy the potter's field as a burial place for foreigners. That is why it has been called the Field of Blood to this day. Then what was spoken by Jeremiah the prophet was fulfilled. "They took the thirty silver coins, the price set on him by the people of Israel, and they used them to buy the potter's field, as the Lord commanded me."

***

It was early morning, and to avoid ceremonial uncleanness, the Jews did not enter the palace; they wanted to be able to eat the

---

Matthew   <u>Mark</u>   *Luke*   **John**

Passover. So Pilate came out to them and asked, "What charges are you bringing against this man?" "If he were not a criminal," they replied, "we would not have handed him over to you." Pilate said, "Take him yourselves and judge him by your own law." "But we have no right to execute anyone," the Jews objected. This happened so that the words Jesus had spoken indicating the kind of death he was going to die would be fulfilled.

And they began to accuse him, saying, "We have found this man subverting our nation. He opposes payment of taxes to Caesar and claims to be Christ, a king." Then Pilate announced to the chief priests and the crowd, "I find no basis for a charge against this man." But the people insisted, "He stirs up the people all over Judea by his teaching. He started in Galilee and has come all the way here." On hearing this, Pilate asked if the man was a Galilean. When he learned that Jesus was under Herod's jurisdiction, he sent him to Herod, who was also in Jerusalem at that time.

When Herod saw Jesus, he was greatly pleased, because for a long time he had been wanting to see him. From what he had heard about him, he hoped to see him perform some miracle. He plied him with many questions, but Jesus gave him no answer. The chief priests and the teachers of the law were standing there, vehemently accusing him. Then Herod and his soldiers ridiculed and mocked him. Dressing him in an elegant robe, they sent him back to Pilate. That day Herod and Pilate became friends – before this they had been enemies.

Pilate called together the chief priests, the rulers, and the people and said to them, "You brought me this man as one who was inciting the people to rebellion. I have examined him in your presence and have found no basis for your charges against him. Neither has Herod, for he sent him back to us as you can see, he has done nothing to deserve death. Therefore, I will punish him and then release him."

When he was accused by the chief priests and the elders, he gave no answer. Then Pilate asked him, "<u>Aren't you going to answer? See</u>

---

how many things they are accusing you of?" But Jesus made no reply, not even to a single charge – to the great amazement of the governor.

Pilate then went back inside the palace, summoned Jesus and asked him, "Are you the king of the Jews?" "Yes, it is as you say," Jesus replied. "Is that your own idea," Jesus asked, "or did others talk to you about me?" "Am I a Jew?" Pilate replied. "It was your people and your chief priests who handed you over to me. What is it you have done?"

Jesus said, "My kingdom is not of this world. If it were, my servants would fight to prevent my arrest by the Jews. But now my kingdom is from another place." "You are a king, then!" said Pilate. Jesus answered, "You are right in saying that I am a king. In fact, for this reason I was born, and for this I came into the world, to testify to the truth. Everyone on the side of truth listens to me." "What is truth?" Pilate asked.

Now it was the governor's custom at the Feast to release a prisoner chosen by the crowd. At that time they had a notorious prisoner called Barabbas in prison with the insurrectionists who had committed murder in the uprising. So when the crowd had gathered; the crowd came up and asked Pilate to do for them what he usually did. Pilate asked them, "Which one do you want me to release to you: Barabbas or Jesus who is called Christ?" For he knew it was out of envy that the chief priests had handed Jesus over to him. But the chief priests and the elders persuaded the crowd to ask for Barabbas and to have Jesus executed. "Which of the two do you want me to release to you?" asked the governor. "Barabbas," they answered. "What shall I do, then, with Jesus who is called Christ?" Pilate asked. *With one voice they cried out all the louder, "Away with this man! Release Barabbas to us!"*

When Pilate was sitting on the judge's seat, his wife sent him this message: "Don't have anything to do with that innocent man, for I have suffered a great deal today in a dream because of him."

Matthew   Mark   *Luke*   **John**

Wanting to release Jesus, Pilate appealed to them again. But they kept shouting, "Crucify him! Crucify him!" For the third time he spoke to them: "Why? What crime has this man committed? I have found in him no grounds for the death penalty. Therefore, I will have him punished and then release him." But with loud shouts they insistently demanded that he be crucified, and their shouts prevailed.

Pilate took Jesus and had him flogged. So the governor's **soldiers took charge of Jesus:** the soldiers took Jesus into the Praetorium and gathered the whole company of soldiers around him. They stripped him and put a <u>purple</u> robe on him, and then wove a crown of thorns and set it on his head. They put a staff in his right hand and knelt in front of him and mocked him. <u>They began to call out to him,</u> "Hail, King of the Jews!" they said. They spit on him and took the staff and struck him on the head again and again. <u>Falling on their knees, they paid homage to him.</u>

Once more Pilate came out and said to the Jews, "Look, I am bringing him out to you to let you know that I find no basis for a charge again him." When Jesus came out wearing the crown of thorns and the purple robe, Pilate said to them, "Here is the man!" As soon as the chief priests and their officials saw him, they shouted "Crucify! Crucify!" But Pilate answered, "You take him and crucify him. As for me, I find no basis for a charge against him." The Jews insisted "We have a law, and according to that law he must die, because he claimed to be the Son of God."

When Pilate heard this, he was even more afraid, and he went back inside the palace. "Where do you come from?" he asked Jesus, but Jesus gave him no answer. "Do you refuse to speak to me?" Pilate said. "Don't you realize I have power either to free you or to crucify you? Jesus answered, "You would have no power over me if it were not given to you from above. Therefore the one who handed me over to you is guilty of a greater sin." From then on, Pilate tried to set Jesus free, but the Jews kept shouting, "If you

---

Matthew   <u>Mark</u>   *Luke*   **John**

let this man go, you are no friend of Caesar. Anyone who claims to be a king opposes Caesar." When Pilate heard this, he brought Jesus out and sat down on the judge's seat at a place known as the Stone Pavement (which in Aramaic is Gabbatha). It was the day of Preparation of Passover Week, about the sixth hour. "Here is your king," Pilate said to the Jews. But they shouted, "Take him away! Take him away! Crucify him!" "Shall I crucify your king?" Pilate asked. "We have no king but Caesar," the chief priests answered. After they had mocked him, they took off the robe and put his own clothes on him. Then they led him away to crucify him. When Pilate saw that he was getting nowhere, but that instead an uproar was starting, *Pilate decided to grant their demand.* He took water and washed his hands in front of the crowd. "I am innocent of this man's blood." *He* said, "It is your responsibility!" All the people answered, "Let his blood be on us and on our children!" <u>Wanting to satisfy the crowd,</u> <u>Pilate</u> released Barabbas to them, *the man who had been thrown into prison for insurrection and murder, the one they asked for, and surrendered Jesus to their will.* He handed him over to be crucified.

Carrying his own cross, he went out. <u>A certain man from Cyrene, Simon, the father of Alexander and Rufus, was passing by on his way in from the country, and they</u> *put the cross on him and forced him to carry it behind Jesus. A large number of people followed him, including women who mourned and wailed for him. Jesus turned and said to them, "Daughters of Jerusalem, do not weep for me; weep for yourselves and for your children. For the time will come when you will say 'Blessed are the barren women, the wombs that never bore and the breasts that never nursed!' Then they will say to the mountains, 'Fall on us!' and to the hills, 'Cover us!' For if men do these things when the tree is green, what will happen when it is dry?"*

Two other men, both criminals, were also led out with him to be executed. They came to a place called Golgotha (which means The Place of the Skull). *They crucified him, along with the criminals – one*

Matthew   <u>Mark</u>   *Luke*   **John**

on his right, the other on his left **and Jesus in the middle.** *Jesus said, "Father, forgive them, for they do not know what they are doing."*

It was the third hour when they crucified him. **Pilate had a notice prepared and fastened to the cross** – above his head they placed the written charge against him: THIS IS JESUS **OF NAZARETH, THE KING OF THE JEWS. Many of the Jews read this sign, for the place where Jesus was crucified was near the city, and the sign was written in Aramaic, Latin, and Greek. The chief priests of the Jews protested to Pilate, "Do not write 'The King of the Jews,' but that this man claimed to be king of the Jews." Pilate answered, "What I have written, I have written."**

When they had crucified him, **the soldiers took his clothes dividing them into four shares, one for each of them, with the undergarment remaining. This garment was seamless, woven in one piece from top to bottom. "Let's tear it," they said to one another. "Let's decide by lot who gets it." This happened that the scripture might be fulfilled which said, "They divided my garments among them and cast lots for my clothing." So this is what the soldiers did.** And sitting down, they kept watch over him there.

Near the cross of Jesus stood his mother, his mother's sister, Mary the wife of Clopas, and Mary Magdalene. When Jesus saw his mother there and the disciple whom he loved standing nearby, he said to his mother, "Dear woman, here is your son," and to the disciple, "Here is your mother." From that time on, this disciple took her into his home.

In the same way, the chief priests, the teachers of the law, and the elders mocked him. "He saved others," they said, but he can't save himself! He's the king of Israel! Let him come down now from the cross, and we will believe in him. He trusts in God. Let God rescue him now if he wants him, for he said, 'I am the Son of God.'"

In the same way the robbers who were crucified with him also heaped insults on him. *The soldiers also came up and mocked him. One of the criminals who hung there hurled insults at him: "Aren't you the Christ? Save yourself and us!" But the other criminal rebuked him. "Don't you fear God," he said, "since you are under the same sentence? We are punished justly, for we are getting what our deeds deserve. But this man has done nothing wrong." Then he said, "Jesus, remember me when you come into your kingdom." Jesus answered him, "I tell you the truth, today you will be with me in paradise."*

It was now about the sixth hour, and darkness came over the whole land until three in the afternoon, for the sun stopped shining. And the curtain of the temple was torn in two from top to bottom. The earth shook and the rocks split. The tombs broke open and the bodies of many holy people who had died were raised to life. They came out of the tombs, and after Jesus' resurrection they went into the holy city and appeared to many people. *Jesus called out with a loud voice,* "Eloi, Eloi, lama sabachthani?" which means, "My God, my God, why have you forsaken me?" When some of those standing by heard this, they said, "<u>Listen,</u> he's calling Elijah." **Later, knowing that all was now completed, and so that the Scripture would be fulfilled, Jesus said, "I am thirsty." A jar of wine vinegar was there, so they soaked a sponge in it, put the sponge on a stalk of the hyssop plant, and lifted it to Jesus' lips.** The rest said, "Now leave him alone. Let's see if Elijah comes to save him." **When he had received the drink, Jesus said, "It is finished."** <u>With a loud cry,</u> *"Father, into your hands I commit my spirit." When he had said this, he breathed his last,* **he bowed his head, and gave up his spirit.**

When the centurion <u>who stood there in front of Jesus</u> and those with him who were guarding Jesus <u>heard his cry and saw how he died,</u> saw the earthquake and all that had happened, they were terrified, and *praised God and said,* "Surely he was *a righteous man,* the Son of God!" *When all the people who had gathered to witness this sight saw what took place, they beat their breasts and went away.*

Matthew   <u>Mark</u   *Luke*   **John**

Now it was the day of Preparation, and the next day was to be a special Sabbath. Because the Jews did not want the bodies left on the crosses during the Sabbath, they asked Pilate to have the legs broken and the bodies taken down. The soldiers therefore came and broke the legs of the first man who had been crucified with Jesus, and then those of the other. But when they came to Jesus and found that he was already dead, they did not break his legs. Instead, one of the soldiers pierced Jesus' side with a spear, bringing a sudden flow of blood and water. The man who saw it has given testimony, and his testimony is true. He knows that he tells the truth, and he testifies so that you also may believe. These things happened so that the scripture would be fulfilled. "Not one of his bones will be broken," and, as another scripture says, "They will look on the one they have pierced."

But all those who knew him, including the women who had followed him from Galilee, stood at a distance, watching these things. Among them were Mary Magdalene, Mary the mother of James <u>the younger</u> and Joses, and <u>Salome</u> the mother of Zebedee's sons. <u>In Galilee these women had followed him and cared for his needs. Many other women who had come up with him to Jerusalem were also there.</u>

As evening approached, there came a rich man from Arimathea, named Joseph, a prominent member of the Council, *a good and upright man who had not consented to their decision and action. He came from the Judean town of Arimathea and he was waiting for the kingdom of God.* **Now Joseph was a disciple of Jesus, but secretly because he feared the Jews.** Going boldly to Pilate, he asked for Jesus' body. Pilate was surprised to hear that he was already dead. Summoning the centurion, he asked him if Jesus had already died. When he learned from the centurion that it was so, he gave the body to Joseph. **He was accompanied by Nicodemus, the man who earlier had visited Jesus at night, brought a mixture of myrrh and aloes: about seventy-five pounds.** Joseph took the body, wrapped it in a clean linen cloth, and

---

placed it in his own new tomb that he had cut out of the rock. **The two of them wrapped it, with the spices, in strips of linen. This was in accordance with Jewish burial customs.** At the place where Jesus was crucified, there was a garden, and in the garden a new tomb, in which no one had ever been laid. **Because it was the Jewish day of Preparation and since the tomb was nearby, they laid Jesus there.** He rolled a big stone in front of the entrance to the tomb and went away. Mary Magdalene and the other Mary were sitting there opposite the tomb.

The women who had come with Jesus from Galilee followed Joseph and saw the tomb and how his body was laid in it. Then they went home and prepared spices and perfumes. But they rested on the Sabbath in obedience to the commandment.

Thurs/Friday

(Matthew 27:57-27:65; Mark 16:1-8;
Luke 22:14-23:56; John 13:1-19:42 [NIV])

15th day of Nisan:

The 15th started the Feast of the Passover day – the lamb was to be eaten that night after it was slain the evening of the 14th. The Passover Sabbath commemorated the occasion when God accepted the blood of the slain lamb placed on the doorposts as the substitute for the death of the firstborn. After Adam and Eve sinned, God slayed an animal and used the skin to cover them – a blood sacrifice. Leviticus 17:11 tells us that life is in the blood. That is why a blood sacrifice was always necessary for forgiveness of sin. That is why Christ had to shed his blood to pay for our sins.

The next day, the one after Preparation Day, the chief priests and the Pharisees went to Pilate. "Sir," they said, "we remember that while he was still alive that deceiver said, 'After three days I will rise again.' So give the order for the tomb to be made secure until the third day. Otherwise, his disciples may come and steal the body and tell the people that he has been raised from the dead. This last deception will be worse than the first."

"Take a guard," Pilate answered. "Go, make the tomb as secure as you know how." So they went and made the tomb secure by putting a seal on the stone and posting a guard.

Matthew   <u>Mark</u>   *Luke*   **John**

Fri/Saturday

16th day of Nisan:

This was the weekly *Sabbath day,* so the women didn't go to the tomb until the following morning. As this second, weekly Sabbath ended at 6 pm, Saturday evening, shops would now open, and the women could buy and prepare what they needed. They purchased the needed spices and prepared them then planned to start off early the next morning for the tomb.

Matthew   Mark   *Luke*   **John**

Sat/Sunday

(Matthew 28:2-4; Mark 16:2-42;
Luke 24:1-41; John 20:1-18 [NIV])

17th day of Nisan

The two disciples on the way to Emmaus state:

> today is the third day since these things were done. (Luke
> 24:21) (NIV)

Counting backwards from Sunday again gives us another proof that
the crucifixion was on Thursday.

When the Sabbath was over, Mary Magdalene, Mary the mother
of James, and Salome bought spices so that they might go to anoint
Jesus' body.

***

There was a violent earthquake, for an angel of the Lord came
down from heaven and, going to the tomb, rolled back the stone and
sat on it. His appearance was like lightning, and his clothes were
white as snow. The guards were so afraid of him that they shook and
became like dead men.

***

Very early on the first day of the week, just after sunrise, while

| Matthew | Mark | Luke | John |

65

it was still dark, *the women took the spices they had prepared and* went to look at the tomb. <u>They asked each other, "Who will roll the stone away from the entrance of the tomb?"</u> But when they <u>looked up, they saw that the stone, which was very large, had been rolled away.</u>

***

So she (Mary of Magdala) came running to Simon Peter and the other disciple, the one Jesus loved, and said, "They have taken the Lord out of the tomb, and we don't know where they have put him!"

***

<u>As they entered the tomb,</u> *they did not find the body of the Lord Jesus. While they were wondering about this, suddenly two men in clothes that gleamed like lightning stood beside them. In their fright the women bowed down with their faces to the ground, but the men said to them, "Do not be afraid, why do you look for the living among the dead? For I know* that you are looking for Jesus <u>the Nazarene,</u> who was crucified. He is not here, he as risen, just as he said. *Remember how he told you while he was still with you in Galilee: 'The Son of Man must be delivered into the hands of sinful men, be crucified, and on the third day be raised again?'" Then they remembered the words.* "Come and see the place where he lay. Then go quickly and tell his disciples <u>and Peter</u>: 'He has risen from the dead and is going ahead of you into Galilee. There you will see him <u>just as he told you.'"</u> <u>Trembling and bewildered,</u> the women hurried away from the tomb, afraid yet filled with joy, and ran to tell his disciples.

***

Matthew	<u>Mark</u>	*Luke*	**John**

... So Peter and the other disciple started for the tomb...

***

While the women were on their way, some of the guards went into the city and reported to the chief priests everything that had happened. When the chief priests had met with the elders and devised a plan, they gave the soldiers a large sum of money, telling them, "You are to say, 'His disciples came during the night and stole him away while we were asleep.' If this report gets to the governor, we will satisfy him and keep you out of trouble." So the soldiers took the money and did as they were instructed. And this story has been widely circulated among the Jews to this very day.

***

When they came back from the tomb, they told all these things to the Eleven and to all the others. It was Mary Magdalene, Joanna, Mary the mother of James, and the others with them who told this to the apostles. But they did not believe the women, because their words seemed to them like nonsense.

***

... both were running, but the other disciple outran Peter and reached the tomb first. He bent over and looked in at the strips of linen lying there but did not go in, *and he went away wondering to himself what had happened.* Then Simon Peter, who was behind him, arrived and went into the tomb. He saw the strips of linen lying there, as well as the burial cloth that had been around Jesus' head. The cloth was folded up by itself, separate from the linen. Finally the other disciple, who had reached the tomb first, also went inside.

| Matthew | Mark | Luke | John |

He saw and believed. (They still did not understand from Scripture that Jesus had to rise from the dead.) Then the disciples went back to their homes, but Mary stood outside the tomb crying.

***

When Jesus rose early on the first day of the week, he appeared first to Mary Magdalene, out of whom he had driven seven demons. As she wept, she bent over to look into the tomb and saw two angels in white, seated where Jesus' body had been, one at the head and the other at the foot. They asked her, "Woman, why are you crying?" "They have taken my Lord away," she said, "and I don't know where they have put him." At this, she turned around and saw Jesus standing there, but she did not realize that it was Jesus. "Woman," he said, "why are you crying? Who is it you are looking for?" Thinking he was the gardener, she said, "Sir, if you have carried him away, tell me where you have put him, and I will get him." Jesus said to her, "Mary." She turned toward him and cried out in Aramaic, "Rabboni!" (which means Teacher). Jesus said, "Do not hold on to me, for I have not yet returned to the Father. Go instead to my brothers and tell them, 'I am returning to my Father and your Father, to my God and your God.'" Mary Magdalene went and told those who had been with him and who were mourning and weeping, *"I have seen the Lord!"* And she told them that he had said these things to her. When they heard that Jesus was alive and that she had seen him, they did not believe it.

Afterward, that same day, two of them were going to a village called Emmaus, about seven miles from Jerusalem. They were talking with each other about everything that had happened. As they talked and discussed these things with each other, Jesus himself appeared in a different form to two of them while they were walking in the country; *but they were kept from recognizing him.*

Matthew   Mark   *Luke*   **John**

He asked them, "What are you discussing together as you walk along?" They stood still, their faces downcast. One of them, named Cleopas, asked him, "Are you only a visitor to Jerusalem and do not know the things that have happened there in these days?" "What things?" he asked. "About Jesus of Nazareth," they replied. "He was a prophet, powerful in word and deed before God and all the people. The chief priests and our rulers handed him over to be sentenced to death, and they crucified him; but we had hoped that he was the one who was going to redeem Israel. And what is more, it is the third day since all this took place. In addition, some of our women amazed us. They went to the tomb early this morning but didn't find his body. They came and told us that they had seen a vision of angels who said he was alive. Then some of our companions went to the tomb and found it just as the women had said, but him they did not see."

He said to them, "How foolish you are, and how slow of heart to believe all that the prophets have spoken! Did not the Christ have to suffer these things and then enter his glory? And beginning with Moses and all the Prophets, he explained to them what was said in all the Scriptures concerning himself.

As they approached the village to which they were going, Jesus acted as if he were going farther. But they urged him strongly, "Stay with us, for it is nearly evening, the day is almost over. So he went in to stay with them.

Sun/Monday

(<u>Mark 16:14;</u> Luke 24:36-43; **John 20:19-25** [NIV])

18th Day of Nisan:

I think the eyes of the two in Emmaus were opened as to who Jesus was when they saw His nail-scarred hands.

When he was at the table with them, he took bread, gave thanks, broke it and began to give it to them. Then their eyes were opened and they recognized him, and he disappeared from their sight. They asked each other, "Were not our hearts burning within us while he talked with us on the road and opened the Scriptures to us?"

They got up and returned at once to Jerusalem. There they found the Eleven and those with them, assembled together and saying, "It is true! The Lord has risen and has appeared to Simon." Then the two told what had happened on the way, and how Jesus was recognized by them when he broke the bread.

While they were still talking about this, **when the disciples were together, with the doors locked for fear of the Jews,** *Jesus himself stood among them and said to them, "Peace be with you." They were startled and frightened, thinking they saw a ghost. He said to them, "Why are you troubled, and why do doubts rise in your minds?"* <u>He rebuked them for their lack of faith and their stubborn refusal to believe those who had seen him after he had risen.</u> *"Look at my hands and my feet. It is I, myself! Touch me and see; a ghost does not have flesh and bones, as you see I have."*

When he had said this, he showed them his hands and feet. And while they still did not believe it because of joy and amazement, he asked them,

---

Matthew   <u>Mark</u>   Luke   **John**

"Do you have anything here to eat?" They gave him a piece of broiled fish and he took it and ate it in their presence. **The disciples were overjoyed when they saw the Lord.** He said to them, "This is what I told you while I was still with you: Everything must be fulfilled that is written about me in the Law of Moses, the Prophets, and the Psalms."

And Jesus said, "Peace be with you! As the Father has sent me, I am sending you." And with that, he breathed on them and said, "Receive the Holy Spirit."

Now Thomas (called Didymus) one of the Twelve, was not with the disciples when Jesus came. So the other disciples told him, "We have seen the Lord!" But he said to them, "Unless I see the nail marks in his hands and put my finger where the nails were and put my hand into his side, I will not believe it."

Later Appearances of Jesus

(Matthew 28:16-20; <u>Mark 16:16-19;</u>
Luke 24:45-53; **John 20:26-21:25** [NIV])

Will our glorified bodies be like Jesus' body at this time? Will we be able to go through locked doors and appear and disappear as needed? Sounds like fun, doesn't it? He was recognized, so I believe we will also be recognized.

Jesus says that those who believe in Him without seeing Him will be blessed. Just think, He's talking about us!

A week later his disciples were in the house again, and Thomas was with them. Though the doors were locked, Jesus came and stood among them and said, "Peace be with you!" Then he said to Thomas, "Put your finger here; see my hands. Reach out your hand and put it into my side. Stop doubting and believe." Thomas said to him, "My Lord and my God." Then Jesus told him, "Because you have seen me, you have believed; blessed are those who have not seen and yet have believed."

Then the eleven disciples went to Galilee, to the mountain where Jesus had told them to go. When they saw him, they worshiped him; but some doubted.

Jesus did many other miraculous signs in the presence of his disciples, which are not recorded in this book. But these are written that you may believe that Jesus is the Christ, the Son of God, and that by believing you may have life in his name.

Afterward Jesus appeared again to his disciples, by the Sea of Tiberias. It happened this way: Simon Peter, Thomas (called Didymus), Nathanael from Cana in Galilee, the sons of Zebedee,

---

Matthew   <u>Mark</u>   *Luke*   **John**

and two other disciples were together. "I'm going out to fish," Simon Peter told them, and they said, "We'll go with you." So they went out and got into the boat, but that night they caught nothing.

Early in the morning, Jesus stood on the shore, but the disciples did not realize that it was Jesus. He called out to them, "Friends haven't you any fish?" "No," they answered. He said, "Throw your net on the right side of the boat and you will find some." When they did, they were unable to haul the net in because of the large number of fish.

Then the disciple whom Jesus loved said to Peter, "It is the Lord!" As soon as Simon Peter heard him say, "It is the Lord," he wrapped his outer garment around him (for he had taken it off) and jumped into the water. The other disciples followed in the boat, towing the net full of fish, for they were not far from shore, about a hundred yards. When they landed, they saw a fire of burning coals there with fish on it and some bread. Jesus said, "Bring some of the fish you have just caught." Simon Peter climbed aboard and dragged the net ashore. It was full of large fish, 153, but even with so many the net was not torn. Jesus said to them, "Come and have breakfast." None of the disciples dared to ask him, "Who are you?" They knew it was the Lord. Jesus came, took the bread and gave it to them and did the same with the fish. This was now the third time Jesus appeared to his disciples after he was raised from the dead.

When they had finished eating, Jesus said to Simon Peter, "Simon, son of John, do you truly love me more than these?" "Yes, Lord," he said, "you know that I love you," Jesus said, "Feed my lambs." Again Jesus said, "Simon son of John, do you truly love me?" He answered, "Yes, Lord, you know that I love you." Jesus said, "Take care of my sheep." The third time he said to him, "Simon son of John, do you love me?" Peter was hurt because Jesus asked him the third time, "Do you love me?" He said, "Lord, you

Matthew   Mark   *Luke*   John

75

know all things; you know that I love you." Jesus said, 'Feed my sheep. I tell you the truth, when you were younger you dressed yourself and went where you wanted; but when you are old you will stretch out your hands, and someone else will dress you and lead you where you do not want to go." Jesus said this to indicate the kind of death by which Peter would glorify God. Then he said to him, "Follow me!"

Peter turned and saw that the disciple whom Jesus loved was following them. (This was the one who had leaned back against Jesus at the supper and had said, "Lord, who is going to betray you?") When Peter saw him, he asked, 'Lord, what about him?" Jesus answered, "If I want him to remain alive until I return, what is that to you? You must follow me." Because of this, the rumor spread among the brothers that this disciple would not die. But Jesus did not say that he would not die; he only said, "If I want him to remain alive until I return, what is that to you?" This is the disciple who testifies to these things and who wrote them down. We know that his testimony is true.

Jesus did many other things as well. If every one of them were written down, I suppose that even the whole world would not have room for the books that would be written.

Then Jesus came to them and said, "All authority in heaven and on earth has been given to me. Therefore, go <u>into all the world</u> and make disciples of all nations, baptizing them in the name of the Father and of the Son and of the Holy Spirit, and teaching them to obey everything I have commanded you. <u>Whoever believes and is baptized will be saved, but whoever does not believe will be condemned. And these signs will accompany those who believe: In my name they will drive out demons; they will speak in new tongues; they will pick up snakes with their hands; and when they drink deadly poison, it will not hurt them at all; they will place their hands on sick people, and</u>

they will get well. And surely I am with you always, to the very end of the age."

Then he opened their minds so they could understand the Scriptures. He told them, "This is what is written: The Christ will suffer and rise from the dead on the third day, and repentance and forgiveness of sins will be preached in his name to all nations, beginning at Jerusalem. You are witnesses of these things. I am going to send you what my Father has promised; but stay in the city until you have been clothed with power from on high." When he had led them out to the vicinity of Bethany, he lifted up his hands and blessed them. After the Lord Jesus had spoken to them, he was taken up into heaven, and he sat at the right hand of God. Then they worshiped him and returned to Jerusalem with great joy. And they stayed continually at the temple, praising God. Then the disciples went out and preached everywhere, and the Lord worked with them and confirmed his word by the signs that accompanied it.

So What? Again I Ask "What Difference Does This Make For You and Me?"

Jesus came for this time to die for us at the moment the Passover lamb was to be slain. He had set all the rules for Passover in Exodus pointing to His substitutionary death for us, and the Scriptures show us that he fulfilled all of the rules.

Does this mean you cannot attend a Good Friday service at your church and be inspired by the service? Absolutely not! You will just realize for yourself the richer, deeper meaning of Jesus' death for you. I can't imagine that God would set these rules and then miss fulfilling them by one day. His death and resurrection mean everything for us, but the fact that His exact fulfillment of the promises He made in the Old Testament makes me realize again how very much he loves us and that I can truly trust Him to exactly fulfill every promise he has made to me – and to you.

Summary of the Last Days

Sat/Sunday
Triumphal Entry
Looked at Temple

Sun/Monday
Cursed Fruitless Fig Tree
Cleansed the Temple

Mon/Tuesday
Withered Fig Tree
Speaks to Religious Leaders about his Authority
Speaks to Disciples about the Fall of Jerusalem and End Time

Tues/Wednesday
Anointed with Perfume
Greeks Seek Jesus
Announces Death
Judas Betrays Jesus
Preparation for Passover

Wed/Thursday
Last Supper
Washes the Disciples Feet
Lord's Supper Instituted
Teaches Disciples on the Way to the Mount of Olives
Tells of the Coming Holy Spirit
Jesus Prays in the Garden
Arrested
Questioned by Annas, Then Caiaphas
Questioned by Pilate, Herod, then Pilate
Sentenced to Death by Crucifixion
After Death, Buried in Joseph of Arimathea's Tomb

Thurs/Friday
Religious Leaders Request the Tomb be Guarded

Fri/Saturday

Sat/Sunday
Women Find the Empty Tomb
Disciples Told of Empty Tomb
Peter and John Go to the Tomb
Jesus Appears to Mary Magdalene
Jesus Appears to Two on the Road to Emmaus

Sun/Monday
Appears to Disciples Without Thomas

Later Appearances
To Disciples With Thomas
To Disciples at Sea of Tiberias
Instructs Peter to Feed His Sheep
Ascension

Interesting Bible Study

<u>List the procedures at Passover from Exodus 12:</u>

A. 12:3 _____ (___) day

B. 12:5_____

C. 12:6 _____(___) day

D. 12:10 _____

E. 12:10 _____

F. 12:13 _____

G. 12:46 _____

<u>Show where procedures were fulfilled:</u>

H. Matt 21:9 _____

I. 2 Cor 5:21 _____

J. Matt 27:46-50 _____

K. Mark 15:42-45 _____

L. (Romans traditionally burned the bodies of criminals after death, but see Matt 27:59&60.)

M. I Peter 1:18 & 19_____

N. John 19:31-37 _____

Answers:

A. Chose lamb – 10th

B. Lamb without blemish

C. Kill in evening - 14th day

   - changed to begin at 3 after tabernacle built

D. Don't let any remain

E. Burn if there are left overs

F. God will pass over when sees blood

G. Don't break any bones

H. Chosen as king or messiah

I. Knew no sin

J. Died at 3 pm

K. Taken down before even

L. Buried

M. Saved by His blood

N. Didn't break his bones – already dead

Some Of my favorite Bible studies

<u>Abraham</u>

<u>Chemistry of the Blood</u>

<u>Everything Points to Christ</u>

<u>The God Who Never Forgets</u>

<u>The Flood</u>

<u>From Adam to Noah</u>

<u>Messianic Line</u>

<u>Theory of Re-Creation</u>

(These represent some of my favorite studies. Remember, I am only a Bible student, not a scholar, so I used the knowledge of several scholars and my Bible to get this information.)

Abraham

Abraham: one of my favorite men in the Old Testament. Once a year our church asked high school students to teach the lesson to adult classes. The lesson I taught was about Abraham sacrificing Isaac. I got so excited about what I learned in the Bible from studying more than just the assigned verses --- but studying what is written elsewhere in the Bible about my subject matter. That was the beginning of my love of Bible study.

Abraham is a great role model for all believers. Romans 4:11 tells us that Abraham is the father of all who believe. Let's see what we can learn from his life to apply to our life.

Genesis 1-11 covers a time period of about 2000 years and deals with the whole human race, where events, not persons, were predominant. That changes after Abraham is born. Now, God is calling out His chosen people. When we begin chapter 12 of Genesis, the focus changes: the main theme is a person. I like learning interesting facts. One is that Noah died a year after Abraham was born. That just blows my mind.

Abraham lived in the city of Ur. Excavations have been made of Ur, and it is very surprising to me what they found. Ur was a very progressive city. Five temples were found – one to the moon god. There were temple-owned factories. One of them produced clothing. Large homes were found: some with three or four rooms. One home was two stories high and had 13 or 14 rooms. Beautiful art pieces were found. Treasures like jewels, a fluted golden tumbler, a golden helmet, gold and silver mounted harps and lyres, and a book about war were found. Excavators also found thousands of small clay tablets. Some had mathematical tables on them. Orders for the construction of canals were found. Amazing! None of this is what I had pictured about the city of Ur or what existed during the days of Abraham. I just envisioned everyone living in tents.

We are told in Genesis 11:31 and 32 that Terah took his son

Abram and his wife Sarai along with Terah's grandson Lot, and they moved to go to Canaan, but instead they settled in Haran along the way. God told Abram to go to a land he would show him and that He would make a great nation from him, and his name would be great. God also told him that He would bless whoever blessed Abram, and curse all who cursed Abram. Abram was 75 years old at the time of his stepping out in faith to follow God's direction. A lesson for us tells us that we're never too old to follow God and live for Him. Abraham didn't know where God was going to lead him. God often gives instructions to us and then He waits until we follow before giving us additional instructions – just as He did with Abram. After we follow, then God leads us to the next step in our walk with Him.

God uses several events in the Bible to help us understand events that occur later. He's such a great writer, that some things mean something for that moment, and then it will also have meaning on a deeper level. We call them a *picture* or a *type*. Abraham's life is filled with types. Abraham's call is a picture or type of our call as believers – the church. We step out in faith from among unbelievers and follow God to the promised land (heaven). Our home is not on earth, it's with God in heaven. We are just journeying through this land to our future home – as Abraham did.

When Abram got to Canaan, he stopped at the tree of Moreh at Shechem. *Moreh* means *instruction* and *Shechem* means *shoulder or strength*. When we are in God's will, we receive strength as we follow God's instructions. The Bible and prayer are where we look for that instruction for our life. Abram built an altar to worship the Lord. Then he moved to Bethel, which means *house of God*. Ephesians 4:22-24 say:

> You were taught, with regard to your former way of life, to put off your old self, which is being corrupted by its deceitful desires; to be made new in the attitude of your minds; and to put on the new self, created to be like God in true righteousness and holiness. (NIV)

If we stay in touch with God through prayer and Bible study, He teaches us the lessons we need in life. God taught Abram, and He wants to teach us as well. We are told that the Lord appeared to Abram and told him that He would give the land to Abram's offspring. This message came with the Canaanites in plain sight, but Abram had faith and knew this would happen. In the same way, we can trust God's Words to us.

Abram was not perfect. Neither are we until we get to heaven. When a famine came, he went to Egypt. (This is the first time Egypt is mentioned in the Bible.) Abram faced the trial of a famine. He did not seek God's counsel, but instead took off for Egypt. He was worried that the Egyptians would kill him because Sarai was beautiful. So, he asked her to lie and say that she was his sister. He forgot that God promised to bless the world through him. How quickly we forget God's promises when we turn our backs on Him. But, fortunately for us, God does not turn His back on us. 2 Timothy 2:13 says:

If we are faithless, he will remain faithful, for he cannot disown himself. (NIV)

Why do you think God allowed the famine to come? We often think that nothing bad will happen to us after we become a Christian, but sin exists in this world, bad things happen. But He can use trials or tragedies in our life to help mold us into the person he desires for us to be – if we ask Him to help us. His desire is for us to grow and learn from our mistakes so that those lessons will prevent later tragedy, and we can now help others who are going through what we went through.

When Abram and Lot left Egypt, they returned to the place between Bethel and Ai where they had stopped before. When Abram arrived there, he built an altar to the Lord – he worshipped the Lord again. But did Lot return and worship the Lord or did he remain in a worldly lifestyle? We all have a choice after we have sinned or faced a problem in life. We can either return to the Lord or turn away from him. We can see from what happens in Abram's life and in Lot's life which is the better choice.

Abram had become very wealthy. Plus, his flocks and Lot's flocks were too much for the land to be able to support them both. Their men became quarrelsome, so Abram suggested they separate. And, not being a selfish man, he let Lot choose first where he wanted to move. Lot is an example of a carnal believer. He had placed his faith in God, but he didn't live that way – he didn't mature in his walk with the Lord. We know Lot was a believer because 2 Peter 2:7 says:

… he rescued Lot, a righteous man …. (NIV)

Lot made his choice based on selfish desires for his best, not seeking God's best. Another lesson for us. We need to seek God's will in decisions we make. God's will for us is always the best choice.

Lot's choice placed him by the city of Sodom where wickedness abounded. When two angels went to his home in the city of Sodom, the perverted men of the town came wanting to have sex with them. How disgusting! Finally, God led Lot out of Sodom before it was destroyed. Another picture that God will deliver his followers before the time of the judgment.

Abram questioned God how he could be the father of many nations when he didn't even have a son. We are told in Genesis 11:30 that Sarai was not able to conceive – some versions of the Bible say she was barren. God said he would have a son, and Abram believed. Abram asked how he would know that he would gain possession of the land. God made a covenant with Abram – the Abrahamic Covenant. This covenant is unique. Most covenants were conditional on something and required both parties to do their part, but this covenant only had one party: God. So it will definitely happen. God told Abram to provide a heifer, a goat, and a ram, each three years old, along with a dove and a young pigeon. They were divided in half, and only God walked through the animals. I know there is meaning in the choice of animals, the age, etc. I'm looking forward to studying that in greater detail.

God changed the name of Abram to Abraham. Abram means *exalted father*, but Abraham means *father of many nations*. When Abraham was 100 years old and Sarah was not able to conceive, Isaac was born. This is a picture to us of the coming Messiah, who also had a miraculous birth.

There is so very much more in Abram's life to learn, but – for the sake of time – I am going to skip much of it. Sarai got her handmaid to sleep with Abram because she was anxious to have that promised son. However, he was not the son God promised. There has been trouble ever since between the descendants of Ishmael and the descendants of Isaac. The lesson learned? We are taught again to wait on God's guidance in order to receive God's best.

Let's look at the hardest test Abraham faced – when God asked him to sacrifice his son Isaac on an altar – the son he had waited for all those years. What would I think? What would you think? We hear nothing of Abraham complaining. He arose early the next morning and left to offer his son – the promised son he had waited on for 25 years – now he cuts the wood to sacrifice that son. He takes two servants with him. Verse 5 of Genesis 22 is the verse that showed me Abraham's complete trust in God. As I shared elsewhere in this book, when I was in high school I was asked to teach an adult Sunday School class. I was assigned to teach the lesson of Abraham offering Isaac. This verse opened my eyes to see the depth of God's provision for us and the beauty of studying His word. We miss so much if we just read a certain passage and don't actually study its meaning.

Genesis 22:5 says:

> He said to his servants, "Stay here with the donkey while I and the boy go over there. We will worship and then we will come back to you." (NIV)

Notice the word *we.* Abraham still trusted God's promise to him.

He knew Isaac was going to return home with him. What faith! His faith was rewarded as we see later. In verse 8, after Isaac asks where the sacrifice was, Abraham says:

> *God himself will provide the lamb for the burnt offering, my son.* (NIV)

I don't think he knew how God would provide, but he still trusted God's promise to him. He continues to tie his son on the altar. God calls to him and says in Genesis 22:12:

> *Do not lay a hand on the boy … Do not do anything to him.* (NIV)

God Himself provided the lamb to be sacrificed for our salvation by providing His son Jesus to pay the price for our sin by shedding his blood upon the cross.

In our Bible study, we should look to see what else we can learn from other parts of the Bible that pertains to what we are studying. Sometimes there are verses listed in the middle of your Bible or in the study notes. Look them up. Look at what we learn about Abraham in Hebrews 11:8-19.

> *By faith Abraham, when called to go to a place he would later receive as his inheritance, obeyed and went, even though he did not know where he was going. By faith he made his home in the promised land like a stranger in a foreign country; he lived in tents, as did Isaac and Jacob, who were heirs with him of the same promise. For he was looking forward to the city with foundations, whose architect and builder is God…. By faith Abraham, even though he was past age – and Sarah herself was barren – was enabled to become a father because he considered him faithful who had made the promise and so from this*

one man, and he as good as dead, came descendants as numerous as the stars in the sky and as countless as the sand on the seashore …. All these people were still living by faith when they died. They did not receive the things promised, they only saw them and welcomed them from a distance …. By faith Abraham, when God tested him, offered Isaac as a sacrifice. He who had received the promises was about to sacrifice his one and only son, even though God had said to him, "It is through Isaac that your offspring will be reckoned." Abraham reasoned that God could raise the dead, and figuratively speaking, he did receive Isaac back from death. (NIV)

What a man! What faith! What a God!

Notes on "The Chemistry of the Blood" by M.R. DeHaan and other studies

God tells us in Leviticus 17:11:

> *For the life of a creature is in the blood, and I have given*
> *it to you to make atonement for yourselves on the altar;*
> *it is the blood that makes atonement for one's life.* (NIV)

M.R. DeHaan was a physician before going into the ministry. That knowledge gave him added insight into this subject. He relates that our bodies are made up of fixed cells, such as muscles, nerves, bones, organs etc. However, our blood is fluid and mobile, so our blood moves throughout the body and supplies these fixed cells with nourishment and carries off waste products. Our blood is pumped by the heart so that the body is constantly supplied and cleansed. This reminds us of the One who made our blood sacrifice. He nourishes us as well. Once the blood fails to reach the cells and parts of the body, they promptly die. If we don't have Christ's atoning blood nourishing us, we die – spiritually and physically.

When Adam ate of the forbidden tree in the Garden of Eden, he died both spiritually and, ultimately, physically. Since life is in the blood, when man died spiritually, something happened to the blood. Sin affected the blood of man, and it became poisonous.

In Acts 17:26, God says:

> *From one man he made every nation of men...* (NIV)

All people are related to one another by the blood of Adam; thus carrying sinful, polluted blood.

This blood carries the sentence of death because of Adam's sin, and – for this reason – all men die a common death. We know that eating from the forbidden tree caused **blood poisoning** and resulted in death. God said, in Genesis 2:16,17:

You are free to eat from any tree in the garden; but you must not eat from the tree of the knowledge of good and evil, for when you eat of it you will surely die. (NIV)

Romans 3:23 says:

For all have sinned and fall short of the glory of God (NIV)

This explains why we are all born sinners The DNA of Adam's sinful blood was passed on through Adam. This poison is so potent that, even after thousands of years, all who are related to Adam die. The only remedy for death is life – provided by the shedding of Christ's sinless blood. The greatest *transfusion* is performed when a sinner – dead in trespasses and sin – is saved by the blood of Christ the moment he believes. The only requisite is faith in the atoning blood of Christ.

DeHaan, with his physician's knowledge, shares that the blood which flows in an unborn babe's arteries and veins developed after the sperm of man has entered the ovum and a fetus begins to develop. Thus, this sinful blood is passed on by man. The mother provides the fetus with the nutritive elements for the building of that little body, but all the blood is formed in the embryo itself. The placenta is constructed in such a way that, although all the soluble nutritive elements such as proteins, fats, carbohydrates, etc. pass freely from mother to child, no actual interchange of a single drop of blood ever occurs normally. God is so amazing. He created mankind in such a way that, when Jesus was born, He would not receive any of this polluted blood. DeHaan listed several medical books supporting this information: Howell's *Textbook of Physiology*, Second Edition, pages 885 and 886; Williams' *Practice of Obstetrics*, Third Edition, page 133; *Nurse's Handbook of Obstetrics* by Louise Zabriskie, R.N., Fifth Edition, page 75; and others.

This explains why Christ could not be born of a man; otherwise he would have had sinful blood. He was born of a virgin through the work of the Holy Spirit, and He was sinless. In Hebrews 2:14 we read:

> Since the children have flesh and blood, he too shared in their humanity so that by his death he might destroy him who holds the power of death – that is, the devil. (NIV)

The word *have* used of mankind means *to share fully* The word referring to Christ, *shared*, means *to take part, but not all.* Conception by the Holy Spirit was the only way that Jesus could avoid being born a sinner. Again, God thinks of everything. Mary nourished the body of Jesus, and He became the seed of David according to the flesh. The Holy Spirit contributed the blood of Jesus. It was sinless blood. It was divine blood. The whole plan of redemption rests upon the power of the sinless blood of Christ on the cross. It was no accident that Jesus died upon a cross. He shed His sinless blood for our atonement. In Revelation we read that the saints of God had washed their robes *white* in the blood of the Lamb. The only way that was possible is because they were washed in the sinless blood of the Lamb.

Remember when God provided clothing for Adam and Eve after they had sinned? This was an example of the atonement of sin by a blood offering. The blood of an animal was shed to get those skins. This was the reason God accepted Abel's sacrifice and not Cain's offering. Abel offered a blood sacrifice from his flock. God required a blood sacrifice for forgiveness of sins. These offerings were only temporary, but pointed to the day when Christ offered His blood sacrifice for us. The offering of Christ's blood is a permanent offering to cover our sins. God tells us in Hebrews 9:22:

> ... without the shedding of blood there is no forgiveness.
> (NIV)

Before the exodus from Egypt, God did not say that he would pass over the children of Israel when he saw how good they were, etc., but he said he would pass over them when he saw the blood on their doorpost. Just as we do not earn our salvation by trying to prove how good we can be. Blood is mentioned about 700 times in the Bible from Genesis to Revelation. In Revelation, we are told about the redeemed throng in heaven. They sing, not about their own goodness, but they sing:

> … *To him who loves us and has freed us from our sins by his blood. Revelation 1:5* (NIV)

Look at these verses:

Revelation 12:10-11:

> *Then I heard a loud voice in heaven say: "Now have come the salvation and the power and the kingdom of our God, and the authority of his Christ. For the accuser of our brother, who accuses them before our God day and night, has been hurled down. They overcame him by the blood of the Lamb and by the word of their testimony….*(NIV)

Ephesians 1:7:

> *In him we have redemption through his blood, the forgiveness of sins, in accordance with the riches of God's grace.* (NIV)

I John 1:9:

> *If we confess our sins, he is faithful and just and will forgive us our sins, and purify us from all unrighteousness.* (NIV)

<u>I John 1:7:</u>

> *But if we walk in the light, as he is in the light, we have*
> *fellowship with one another, and the blood of Jesus, his*
> *Son, purifies us from all sin. (NIV)*

Although Jesus' body was in the tomb in death for three days and three nights, no corruption entered because he contained incorruptible blood. I Peter 1:18,19 say:

> *For you know that it was not with perishable things*
> *such as silver and gold that you were redeemed from*
> *the empty way of life handed down to you from your*
> *forefathers, but with the precious blood of Christ, a lamb*
> *without blemish or defect. (NIV)*

Hebrews 9:24-26 say:

> *For Christ did not enter a man-made sanctuary that*
> *was only a copy of the true one; he entered heaven itself,*
> *now to appear for us in God's presence. Nor did he enter*
> *heaven to offer himself again and again, the way the*
> *high priest enters the Most Holy Place every year with*
> *blood that is not his own. Then Christ would have had*
> *to suffer many times since the creation of the world. But*
> *now he has appeared once for all at the end of the ages*
> *to do away with sin by the sacrifice of himself. (NIV)*

As the hymn says, "There is a fountain filled with blood, drawn from Immanuel's veins; and sinners plunged beneath that flood, lose all their guilty stains!"

As the Bible tells us – "Life is in the blood." Christ offered His sinless blood to pay for our sin. "Thank you Jesus!"

My mother always taught me that the Bible was a bottomless

treasure chest. From this study, we can see an example of that. If we just allow God to lead us in the study of His Word, there are innumerable wonders to discover.

Keep digging!

Everything Points to Christ

Both the Tabernacle and the Feasts of the Old Testament point to Christ, His coming, His crucifixion, the rapture, the judgment, and then eternal life with Him in heaven. I simply do not understand how anyone can view the Bible as 66 individual books and not see the continuity throughout. It was written by 40 authors over a period of 1500 years with no contradictions and one story running throughout: the story of redemption of sinful mankind.

2 Timothy 3:16 says:

> *All Scripture is God-breathed and is useful for teaching,*
> *rebuking, correcting, and training in righteousness, ...*
> *(NIV)*

God wrote his book, the Bible, to tell his story of redemption of sinful man from the beginning to the end of the Bible. I remember hearing M.R. DeHaan saying if you don't see Jesus on a page of the Bible, you need to read it again.

Both the furniture used in the Temple (or Tabernacle) and the feasts were exactly planned out by God – as well as the ark built by Noah. Everything has a meaning for us, which we see as we study. Similarly, God is the one who set out the rules for the plan of our salvation, and he is the one who seeks us out individually to save us.

I learned much from the book, Charting the Bible Chronologically: A Visual Guide to God's Unfolding Plan. It is written by Ed Hinson and Thomas Ice.

The Seven Feasts

Leviticus 23:1 & 2 state:

> The Lord said to Moses, "Speak to the Israelites and say
> to them: 'These are my appointed feasts; the appointed
> feasts of the Lord, which you are to proclaim as sacred
> assemblies.'"(NIV)

As we will see, each feast had a special meaning. Consequently,
they were to be followed exactly as God stated.

The Sabbath: This is not included in the seven feast days because
it was a weekly gathering of His people and there was no sacrifice to
be offered. It was celebrated at home, not in Jerusalem as the others
were. It was a day of rest for the Jewish people, and they were not
to work. It commemorated the fact that the Lord rested after the
creation of the world. As mentioned in the book above, the Sabbaths
involved with these feasts were not on the 7th-day Sabbath, but were
special Sabbaths, holy days for sacred assemblies. We know that
because there were special Sabbaths on the 1st, 10th, 15th, and 22nd of
Nisan. Those days are not seven days apart. On each of these special
Sabbaths, the Jewish people were to do no work.

This leads me to think this compares with the fact that God
wants us to rest in Him, trust Him, and spend time with Him. Our
life is blessed when we do.

The Passover Feast: This feast had it's origin in Egypt when the
Children of Israel were delivered from their slavery to the Egyptians.
A lamb without blemish was to be selected and slain on the 14th day
of that month. We all can see the meaning of this. As we are told in
I Corinthians 5:7:

Christ, our Passover Lamb, has been sacrificed. (NIV)

Notice that each feast is in the same sequence as our salvation experience. First, Jesus was crucified on the 14th day of Nisan, paying the price for our sins.

The Feast of Unleavened Bread: This began on the 15th day of Nisan at the beginning of that day, after the Passover lamb was slain on the 14th. The Jewish day began at evening, so after the lamb was slain, this feast immediately followed and continued for a week during which the Jewish people could only eat unleavened bread. Leaven in the Bible is a picture (or "type") of sin. In Luke 12:1, Jesus tells His disciples:

> ... *Be on your guard against the yeast* (leaven) *of the Pharisees, which is hypocrisy. (NIV)*

That is the reason the Jewish people were to rid their homes of leaven during this celebration, signifying ridding ourselves of sin. Once we have accepted Christ's sacrifice to pay for our sins, then during our walk with Christ, we are to begin growing in our walk with the Lord and getting rid of sin in our life, which we can only do through the power of the Holy Spirit who lives within us. Immediately after our salvation, we begin our walk with Jesus – just as the Feast of Unleavened Bread begins immediately after the Passover and continued for a week. Our salvation happens at that moment we accept Christ as our Savior, but our walk with Him is longer. During that time, we are to rid ourselves of the leaven (sin) in our lives.

The Feast of First Fruits: This feast took place on the day after the Feast of Unleavened Bread. The Israelites were to take an offering from all they had received from God – their wheat, their fruit, their animals – and make an offering of thanksgiving for all

He has provided and acknowledging their dependence upon Him. The priest was to wave a sheaf of the first grain before the Lord. This signifies Jesus' resurrection from the dead. I Corinthians 15:20 says:

> But Christ has indeed been raised from the dead, the firstfruits of those who have fallen asleep. (NIV)

The Feast of Pentecost: This feast occurred 50 days after the Feast of First Fruits, which celebrated the first of the crop. The Feast of Pentecost celebrated the result of the crop – not just the ingathering of the crop, but grain which had been ground into flour and then baked into the two loaves. Plus, seven lambs, one bullock, and two rams were to be offered with the loaves. This feast points to the fact that both Jews and Gentiles were being brought into God's kingdom. The church was established on this day. It was on Pentecost that the Holy Spirit entered the disciples, and they began to preach and invite all into the kingdom.

The first four feasts happened in the spring. Spring represents newness and beginning. There are three more feasts, and they occur in the fall. Fall represents the ending. The interval between the spring feasts and the fall feasts was four months. It represents this current time where the church is being called out. I Corinthians 12:13 says:

> For we were all baptized by one Spirit so as to form one body – whether Jew or Gentile ....." (NIV)

The Feast of Trumpets: This feast was to be celebrated on the 1st day of the 2nd month and started the second series of feasts. The Jewish people were to blow trumpets at the beginning of this celebration. Numbers 10:1-10 describe what was to happen. I can't think about trumpets without thinking about the rapture. There were two trumpets blown at the Feast of Trumpets. In our Biblical timeline, we are at the end of the calling out of believers. Next will be the rapture when the trumpet is blown. I Corinthians 15:52 states:

For the trumpet will sound, the dead will be raised imperishable, and we will be changed. (NIV)

Yay! We will leave this evil world and go be with the Lord. To the Jews, the first trumpet meant calling together an assembly, but the second trumpet signified a time to move. It seems this second trumpet refers to the calling out of "the elect" to return to Israel. *Mark 13:26 & 27 say:*

At that time men will see the Son of Man coming in clouds with great power and glory. He will send his angels and gather his elect from the four winds, from the ends of the earth to the ends of the heavens. (NIV)

Read also Deuteronomy 30:3-5; Isaiah 43:6; Jeremiah 32:27; Ezekiel 34:13 and 36:24.

The Day of Atonement: This was the annual day each year the Jewish people were to bring offerings to pay for their sins. This either refers to the period of the judgment upon people who turned their back upon the Lord, or this may refer to when the Jewish elect return and they repent. Zechariah 12:10 tells us:

And I will pour out on the house of David and the inhabitants of Jerusalem a spirit of grace and supplication. They will look on me, the one they have pierced, and they will mourn for him as one mourns for an only child, and grieve bitterly for him as one grieves for a firstborn son. (NIV)

The Feast of Tabernacles: This feast was to be held at the end of the harvest. The Jewish people would dwell in booths to remind them that they lived in booths when God delivered them from Egypt. It is believed that this feast refers to the time after the Second Coming when we will all tabernacle (or live) together with the Lord.

I definitely need more study on this subject. It is important enough that God put it in His Word, so He wants us to study it and learn from it.

I am just amazed when I see that if we will just take the time, we'll see additional things that God is telling us. How sad if we don't take the time to look.

The Tabernacle and Temple

Just as there were seven feasts, there were exactly seven pieces of furniture in the Temple which speak of God's perfection or completion. DeHaan, in his book *The Tabernacle,* points out that the Tabernacle was the perfect type or picture of the Lord Jesus Christ and His work. Read Hebrews 9.

If you stood on the outside of the Temple, you would not guess how beautiful the inside was. On the outside you would not see the gold-plated vertical boards. The walls were covered with gold. People on the outside represent the sinner. The priest on the inside represents the believer who has passed through the door. Jesus tells us in John 10:9:

> *I am the gate (door); whoever enters through me will be saved. (NIV)*

Once we are inside, we are safe. Remember Noah? Once he was inside the ark, he was safe: another picture God gives us. This verse also points out that Jesus is the only way of salvation. Some say we are just saying trusting in Christ alone is the only way because we're elitist. God, Jesus, and the Holy Spirit created this world, and they knew the only way of salvation. We evangelize because we want others to be saved as well. Also, God charges us with that responsibility. II Peter 3:9 says,

> *He is patient with you, not wanting anyone to perish, but everyone to come to repentance.*

Satan tries to mimic all that Christ has done to keep people confused and from trusting in Him. John 10:28 -30, my favorite verses, say:

*I give them eternal life, and they shall never perish, no
one can snatch them out of my hand. My Father, who
has given them to me, is greater than all; no one can
snatch them out of my Father's hand. I and the Father
are one. (NIV)*

Why are these my favorite verses? I use hand motions to explain why. Open one hand which represents Jesus. We are safe inside His hand as the verse says. But, open the other hand. The verse tells us that no one can snatch us from God's hand either. When you place one hand on top of the other, since Jesus and God are one, we see how very safe we are in their hands. This also tells us that once we are saved, no one can snatch us away.

The first article of furniture seen upon entering the Temple was the **altar**. The blood of an animal was poured out at the base of the altar. Of course, we learned earlier that the Bible says *life is in the blood*. The shed blood of an innocent animal was necessary and represents Christ's shed blood as a sacrifice for us to receive the gift of eternal life.

Next we see the **laver** which is for cleansing. We must be clean to be in the presence of God. We receive that cleansing when we accept Christ's gift of salvation. He shed his sinless blood in order to clean us who have sinful blood. The laver also shows that we are separating ourselves from the sins of this world.

Next is the **table of shewbread**, a place of fellowship. During the time we spend on earth, we are to spend it fellowshipping with other believers, but mostly fellowshipping with Christ. We do that through prayer and Bible study. God desires to fellowship with us. He loves us. After our salvation and we are cleansed, we have the privilege of coming closer to God. How blessed we are.

The **altar of incense or lampstand** is next. M.R. DeHaan, in his book *The Tabernacle* states: "*We who have been saved by the blood at the altar, cleansed by the Word at the laver, drawn into fellowship at the table, fed by the Word of God, are now ready to let our light shine in* testimony." We have been left on earth for this work – to testify to the sinful world in the hope of their accepting salvation. We could have been taken to heaven immediately after becoming a Christian, but God wants us to be a light in this dark, sinful world and lead others to him.

Next is the **golden incense altar**, the symbol of prayer and intercession. Then we go through the veil to the most holy place, leading us to the **ark of the covenant** which exemplifies our complete surrender to Christ. Lastly, there is the **mercy seat**, where we, according to DeHaan, find *perfect peace and complete victory and rest*.

Please continue to study the meaning of these items that represent our Christian walk with the Lord. Let's keep looking for the lessons God wants to teach us.

1 have to confess that I don't always study in depth, but see what there is to learn when we spend more time studying God's Word.

The God Who Never Forgets: Lessons From Joseph
(A Bible study from Our Daily Bread)

Joseph was in the prison in Egypt for a divine appointment. In Genesis 40:1, the pieces of the puzzle begin to come together. Two of Pharaoh's officials – his royal butler and his royal baker – offended the king. These were not just household servants. In ancient times of palace intrigue and political assassinations, it was absolutely critical that these men be totally loyal. Somehow (and we know it was at God's bidding) they had failed Pharaoh, so they were placed in the prison where Joseph was the head steward. Verses 2 & 3 say:

> *Pharaoh was angry with his two officials, the chief cupbearer and the chief baker, and put them in custody in the house of the captain of the guard, in the same prison where Joseph was confined. (NIV)*

God is in Control of our Lives. Nothing Happens by Accident:

Notice who entrusted the butler and baker to Joseph's care. It was the captain of the guard – Potiphar (verses 4 & 37:36). Joseph accepted the responsibility and began the task of serving these disgraced members of Pharaoh's court. This was not just some accident that happened. It was a divine appointment. It is so important for us to notice this fact and realize the same thing happens to us in our life. There is no such thing as a coincidence with God. He is in control of every aspect of our lives. Nothing happens by accident. Everything occurs for a reason.

One of the greatest joys in our life is to look expectantly for the hand of God in all of the circumstances of life:

We need to look expectantly for the hand of God in all of the circumstances of our life. Joseph and these two prisoners ended up in prison at the same time – that was no accident. They were right on schedule for the perfect plan of God, even though they certainly would not have chosen this plan for their lives.

Here's something important to notice. Joseph had become sensitive to others. He had previously lacked this characteristic. Look at Genesis 37. Joseph definitely didn't have the gift of humility or concern for the feelings of others. In Genesis 40:6-7, we learn that Joseph recognized their hurt and distress. It would have been easy to simply turn away and think to himself that no one seemed to be concerned about what he was dealing with and then wonder why no one seemed to be concerned about how he was being treated – how he was being mistreated. It would have been easy for Joseph to think, *Why should I care about them? Who cares about me?* But, instead, Joseph accepted the disappointment of unjust imprisonment. Joseph didn't allow his circumstances to change his relationship with God. He didn't allow his hurt to prevent him from noticing the hurt others must have felt. Joseph could have ignored the butler and the baker, but he didn't. He had the grace to set aside his personal adversity and help others who were hurting. Our lives are filled with disappointment and loss, but we can be overcomers by refusing to become self-absorbed and self-centered. Instead of wasting our energy in self-pity, we can invest our time in meeting the needs of others.

Joseph interpreted the dreams of the two officials (40:8-19), making sure they knew that he was not the one who deserved the credit – but God. His trust was in the Lord, not in himself. What a contrast to what he was before with his brothers when he lorded his dreams over them. Now his trust was in the Lord. After Joseph interpreted the butler's dream, he asked only that he would not forget him (40:14-15).

Earlier, Joseph's purity was rewarded with imprisonment. Now, his caring was paid back by insensitivity. Nothing happened for two full years. Joseph was abandoned by the butler, not by people who were his enemies. It would have been easy for him to crumble and be disillusioned and disappointed in God as often happens today. But, we remain faithful since our trust is in God and not in man. Even though the butler had forgotten Joseph; God hadn't. At times like this, we need to learn the indispensable character quality of patient trust.

Pharaoh was finally out of options when he needed someone to interpret his dream, so he called for Joseph. The cupbearer had finally remembered Joseph and told Pharoah about him. We see another vital principle – godly character is unaffected by the harsh circumstances of life. Undiminished by unfair treatment and years in prison, Joseph stepped forward with three qualities he had learned through the years:

Dignity: Egyptians were clean shaven. Joseph shaved and changed his clothes. Joseph dressed appropriately to go before the king. He had a sense of propriety and decorum that years in prison could not erase.

Humility: Joseph didn't use the situation to promote himself or exalt himself as he had done earlier in life with his family. (Gen 37:5-10). In spite of all that had happened, he learned to put his trust in the Lord and not in himself. We need to learn the same lesson.

Faith: Joseph knew God would give him an answer to interpret Pharaoh's dream. Daniel, in Daniel 2:27-30, and Paul, in Acts 26, said the same thing hundreds of years later.

These characteristics remind me of my deceased husband, Harold Ellis. He founded JAIL Ministry in Belton, Texas. JAIL stands for *Jesus Acts in Inmates Lives*. He went into prisons across the country, but mostly here at home. He was as much at home with those guys in prison as he was with wealthy people when he asked for their financial support to help the ministry. He was definitely a very special person.

Again I say that we are so blessed when we spend time studying God's Word. Cross reference the Scripture. You'll learn even more. I hope this was as much a blessing for you as it was for me.

The Flood

I get some wild ideas sometimes. Plus, I'm a visual learner. I like to see things in print. Here's one of my latest ideas. One day I decided to make a chart of the people who lived at the same time as Adam. On the left side of my chart, I listed years – one hundred years apart. Then I read who lived after Adam and put the years they were born and when they died.

I realized the flood took place in 1656. The Bible tells us that Noah was 600 years old when the flood came. (Genesis 7:11) I love learning facts like these, don't you?.

The chart I made appears on the following page.

From Adam to Noah

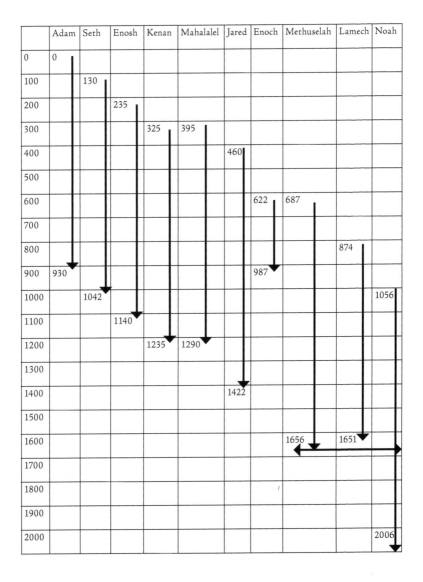

Noah and the Ark

These notes are mainly from the book: *In Search of Noah's Ark* by Dave Balsiger and Charles E Sellier Jr.

The story of Noah begins in chapter 6 of Genesis. We are introduced to some sinful people. Verse 2 mentions "the sons of God." There are different opinions about who they are, but I agree with the one that says that the "sons of God" refer to angels – the fallen angels who followed Satan in his rebellion against God. A word study through the Bible of the phrase "sons of God" seems to give us the definition that they are beings created directly by God – such as angels and Adam. See Job 1:6, 2:1, and 38:7. It appears that this was another of Satan's attempts to defeat God by attempting to defile the Messianic bloodline.

What a mighty flood! If all of the water vapor in our atmosphere turned into rain, it would cover less than two inches. So, what caused there to be enough rain to cover the highest mountains by twenty feet? Again, we know the Bible is God's true Word. When we have a problem understanding, study and see if we can find the answer. We'll never be able to understand everything in the Bible, but we can study and read the words of people who have studied a certain subject. There will be many opinions we cannot trust. Some just say the Bible cannot be trusted. We can immediately mark that person's opinion off our list because the Bible was written by God through men. Others will say it's just a story designed to teach us a lesson and the details are not important. Again, mark that person off your list because we know all of God's Word is true and fits together. See if the person's words that we are reading from shows that every word is true and can show how it fits with other verses in the Bible. If so, then we can trust that writer. The Bible is one story, not a lot of individual stories. There is no contradiction, so all must fit together. Here is what I learned from the book *In Search of Noah's Ark* by Charles E Sellier and Dave Balsiger.

Many scientists who have studied the flood feel that the flood was caused by more than rainfall and that the pre-flood earth was much different than the world today. They feel it existed in a greenhouse effect – a permanent, thick cloud cover. It may have been similar to the canopy surrounding the planet Venus. It is assumed that the pre-flood atmosphere held three to five times as much water vapor as today. The canopy was probably three to five thousand feet thick and about five to ten thousand feet above sea level. The effects of such a covering would be that the temperature around the entire earth would be very much the same everywhere because the sun's rays could not penetrate directly onto the earth's surface. Consequently, there would not be the extreme difference in heat and cold as exists today. Since that is true, there would be no planetary wind system. Since wind causes rain, it would not have rained. Read Genesis 2:5-6. That seems to tell us the earth was watered by dew.

Geology supports this view because many desert areas (such as the Sahara Desert) have been found which geologists state were at one time a swampy, humid area. If this theory is true, another result would be that people would live much longer, as seen previously in the *From Adam to Noah* chart. People lived much longer lives than we do now. They lived to be about nine hundred years old. Then, in Abraham's day, the life expectancy was only about one hundred fifty years. Today, that number has dropped to about seventy years. What a difference!

In Genesis 7:11 we are told that:

> … *all the springs of the great deep burst forth, and the floodgates of the heavens were opened.* (NIV)

From this we learn that the water of the flood came first from the depths of the earth and then the rains fell. Some scientists believe that a great, violent chain reaction took place under the canopy and may have been started by the eruption of the heated and pressurized water existing under the earth's thin crust – possibly a chain of volcanic eruptions. If so, vast amounts of dust would be blown skyward, and the process of condensation would begin and then rain would fall from the vast canopy.

Another possibility is that a giant meteor or many huge meteors crashed through the canopy causing the rays of the sun to penetrate the earth's atmosphere which, too, would bring about the same conditions of atmospheric violence. Of course, whatever happened, it was all under the direction of God who had previously announced the event to Noah. (See Genesis 6:17)

If there were a world-wide flood, there should be geological evidence to find. And there is. It is estimated that more than 75% of the earth's surface is sedimentary in nature. Sediment – in the dictionary – is defined as material that settles to the bottom in a liquid. India has been discovered to be the deepest known sedimentary area with deposits 60,000 feet deep. Many, many sedimentary deposits have been found where fossilized remains of animals, plants, and man-made artifacts exist – often from far different geological regions, appearing to have been dumped together. Fossils of fish and other sea animals have been found at the tops of several mountains, including Mt. Everett. In some areas, large numbers of fossils have been found which make it clear that the animal, mostly fish, suffered an extremely violent, yet sudden death.

This event would have been traumatic enough that Noah and his descendants would continue to talk about it, so it seems many nations would have a record of a story of a flood. This story would now be approximately 5,000 years old. And a story of a great flood has been found in more than 200 different cultures, such as the Eskimos, Russia, Finland, Iceland, New Zealand, etc. The accounts differ, as would any story told and retold by descendants over thousands of years. It appears native beliefs were added to the stories, but every one of them had these facts in common:

1. Mankind was destroyed for moral reasons;
2. One man was warned of the impending flood;

3. Everyone who was not on the boat was destroyed, and all of today's present population descended from those who were spared because of being on the boat; and

4. Each account mentions the involvement of animals; sometimes about their being on board and, oftentimes, birds are mentioned.

It is very interesting to note that all countries that tell about the boat landing say that it landed in their own country. There is only one country that tells about the boat landing but say it landed in another country. That country was the story written by the Hebrews. That, too, leads us to believe that this one is the true story. It was God who wrote the story through Bible writers. That is the real reason we know it is true.

Genesis 6:14-16 give the directions God gave Noah about building the ark. The dimensions were 450' long by 75' wide by 45' high. The shape of this ship was such as to make it slow-moving, because the length was six times the width. Many vessels today which move freight are built with similar dimensions of length to width. A scale model replica has been built using these dimensions and then tested. The results showed that this was the best shape and size for safety in a bad storm. The boat being tested was impossible to capsize. Naturally, because God designed the ark.

Genesis 6:20 and 7:8,15, and 16 tell us that Noah did not have to go gather the animals which entered the ark. How? God must have placed some instinct of nature in them similar to their migrating instincts of today. How did animals co-exist with Noah and his family? The reduced lighting, restricted movement, and the rocking movement of the ark would cause an even greater amount of hibernation. Possibly God caused a great change in the nature of the animals. However God did it, He is the one who made it all happen.

Here is the timetable on board the ark:

10th day of the 2nd month – went into the ark

17th day of the 2nd month – rain began

26th day of the 3rd month – rain stopped (after 40 days)

17th day of the 7th month – ark rested on the mountain (after 150 days)

1st day of the 10th month – mountain tops seen

10th day of the 11th month – raven and dove sent out

17th day of the 11th month – dove brought olive leaf back

24th day of the 11th month – dove didn't return

1st day of the 1st month – removed cover

27th day of the 2nd month – left the ark

Noah and his family spent one year and seventeen days on board the ark.

The Lessons We Learn from the Days of Noah

(These notes are taken from the book, *The Days of Noah* by M.R. DeHaan

I love M.R. DeHaan. I grew up listening to him around the dinner table. While we ate together, DeHaan was speaking on the radio. What a blessing he was for our family. Here are a few of his insights into the time of Noah. I was fortunate enough to meet DeHaan's son, Richard DeHaan. He was also a special Christian man.

DeHaan points out that God always tells His own about what will happen in the future. God has made it clear what our future holds if we are His child. Next will be the rapture and then the tribulation. Both of those events are pictured in the Old Testament through what is called a *picture* or *type*. DeHaan goes into much greater detail than I can do here. God wants us to know His plan for the future. Matthew 24:37 is an example of God using one event to further explain an event that will occur later.

Before Jesus was arrested and died on the cross, He took his disciples aside and told them that He would return. When the disciples asked for a sign of when Jesus would return, He said to them in Matthew 24:37-39:

> *As it was in the days of Noah, so it will be at the coming of the Son of Man. For in the days before the flood, people were eating and drinking, marrying and giving in marriage, up to the day Noah entered the ark, and they knew nothing about what would happen until the flood came and took them all away. That is how it will be at the coming of the Son of Man. (NIV)*

Chapters 4, 5, and 6 of Genesis show us what conditions existed before the flood and will exist before the second coming. Chapter

4 talks about people's belief about God; chapter 5 shows us the different groups of people *during the time;* and chapter 6 introduces us to disgusting sex life of the people. Jesus also states that no one will know the exact date of His return, but he does tell us to study the signs from Genesis to know when the second coming is near.

<u>Chapter 4</u> tells us about Cain and Abel. They represent two different types of *Christians.* After Adam and Eve sinned, God demonstrated for them the proper offering for atonement of sin. This has been covered in the article on the chemistry of the blood. The shedding of blood is a requirement for an acceptable offering to God. You might ask whether or not Adam and Eve had told Cain and Abel the correct sacrifice. Look at Hebrews 11:4:

> By **faith** Abel offered God a better sacrifice than Cain did. By faith he was commended as a righteous man, when God spoke well of his offerings. And by faith he still speaks, even though he is dead. (NIV)1

I believe they did tell their children about offering a sacrifice of blood for the atonement of sin. It was Cain's idea to present an offering to God. Where did he learn of presenting an offering to God if not from his parents? However, his offering consisted of the results of his work to produce the fruit he offered. Cain and Abel represent the difference in two groups who claim to be Christians. One group thinks they need to work and do good things to be acceptable to God. The Bible says otherwise. It is only by faith in God's sinless, blood sacrifice of Jesus shedding His blood on the cross. We see the contrast of man's way by works and God's way by faith in Christ. I have to wonder if the killing of Abel by his brother Cain is a picture of the intense hatred other religions have for us as Christians and their attempt to kill us?

Here is DeHaan's description: *Who can deny that the outstanding religious development of today is the conflict between the liberals and the true evangelicals. . . . The line of demarcation is becoming more definite.*

We must take our stand with one or the other. Either we follow the way of Cain, the popular way, by compromising the fundamentals of the faith and join the parade of ecumenicism toward the great world church, or we take our stand with Abel in a minority group, despised and opposed on every hand. The gap between the two has widened until it is becoming impossible to ride the fence, and we must take a stand either with the religious descendants of Cain or the spiritual generation of Abel.

Just as the wickedness of the pre-flood days brought on the judgment of God, so it will be repeated just before the coming again of Jesus. . . . The rise of a liberal theology, which under the guise of tolerance says that faith in the virgin birth, the deity of Christ, the substitutionary atonement by blood, the bodily resurrection of Jesus, and His literal coming again are not essential, and that the Bible is not verbally inspired and the record of the first chapters of Genesis including the story of Cain and Abel are not to be taken literally but are only an allegory – this rise of modern theology, I say, is one of the foremost significant signs of the coming of Christ. The apparent victory of modernism in the way of Cain, and the apparent decline in the number of 'true to the core' fundamentalists is a repeat of the story of Cain and Abel.

It's heartbreaking when we hear people we love state that the Bible is just a bunch of stories which are not true. Jude 11 says:

> Woe to them! They have taken the way of Cain; they
> have rushed for profit into Balaam's error; they have
> been destroyed in Korah's rebellion. (NIV)

I know these people are hard to witness to because they see us as people who are misguided. But, we can pray for them that they will someday see the light of God's Word.

Chapter 5 of Genesis introduces us to the three classes of people alive before the flood: Enoch was taken to heaven before the flood, Noah and his family were spared by God through the flood, and the final group refers to those who died in the flood.

The man taken to heaven before the flood was Enoch. Jude 14 and 15 tell us about him:

> *Enoch, the seventh from Adam, prophesied about these men: "See, the Lord is coming with thousands upon thousands of his holy ones to judge everyone, and to convict all the ungodly of all the ungodly acts they have done in the ungodly way, and of all the harsh words ungodly sinners have spoken against him...."*

Enoch prophesied about the judgment, the flood. When Enoch was 65 years old, he had a son, Methuselah. Methuselah's name means, "When he is dead, it shall be sent." Methuselah died in 1656 B.C. – the same year as the flood. God always lets His children know the future. See Psalm 25:14. In Genesis 5, we read that Enoch walked with God, and God took him – he was raptured. Thus, Enoch represents believers in Christ who will be raptured before the judgment.

In Luke 17:26-30, Jesus compares the end time to the days of Lot. In II Peter 2:7, we learn that Lot was a believer; however, he was a carnal Christian. Read his story to see the moral decay he lived with. God delivered him before the destruction of Sodom and Gomorrah because he was a believer. This tells me that Christians, God's children, whether strong believers or carnal believers, will be delivered before the tribulation in the rapture.

<u>Chapter 6</u> is where we learn of the time when the fallen angels married women on earth and produced monstrosities. This may have been Satan's plan to defeat the possibility of a promised seed, an unblemished seed, coming to save mankind. This chapter tells us that a sign of the times before the return of Christ will be sexual immorality. We cannot deny that is prevalent in our world today. Divorce, unfaithfulness, and sexual deviants seem to be more and more commonplace in our society today.

One of the things I learn from all this information (besides the fact that the rapture will come before the tribulation) is that the Bible is one complete story. The Old and New Testaments are linked together to tell us God's message.

The Messianic Line

God
Adam
Seth
Enos
Cainan
Mahalalel
Jared
Enoch
Methuselah
Lamech
Noah
Shem
Arphaxad
Cainan
Shelah
Eber
Peleg
Reu
Serug
Nahor
Terah
Abraham
Isaac
Jacob
Judah
Perez
Hezron
Rama
Amminadab
Nahshon
Salmon
Boaz
Obed
Jesse
David

Matthew's List:	Luke's List:
written to the Jews –	(written to the Greeks – (Gentiles)
(presents Jesus as king)	(presents Jesus as the perfect man)

Solomon	Nathan
Rehoboam	Mattatha
Abijah	Melea
Asa	Eliakim
Jehoshaphat	Jonan
Jehoram	Joseph
Uzziah	Judah
Jotham	Simeon
Ahaz	Levi
Hezekiah	Matthat
Manasseh	Jorim
Amon	Eliezer
Josiah	Jose
Jeconiah *(note on next page)	Er
(exile to Babylon)	Elmodam Maath
Shealtiel	Cosam
Zerubbabel	Addi
Abiud	Melchi
Eliakim	Neri
Azor	Shealtiel
Zadok	Zerubbabel
Akim	Rhesa
Eliud	Joanan
Eleazar	Joda
Mattham	Josech
Jacob	Semein
Joseph, (the husband of Mary)	Mattathlas
	Maath
	Naggai
	Esli
	Nahum
	Amos
	Mattathias
	Joseph
	Jannai
	Melki
	Levi
	Matthai
	Heli (Heli was the father of Mary)

*See Jer. 22:24-30: Jechonias/Coniah, was very evil & was told by God that none of his descendants would prosper or sit on the throne of David – notice Jesus' lineage did not come through this line.

SOLOMON	NATHAN
succeeded David on the throne - **kingly** right to the throne came through him	was David's oldest son when David died had the **legal** right to the throne

NOTES:

Look at these clues in the Old Testament about Christ's lineage:

Genesis 3:15	From the seed of woman
Genesis 9:26,27	Line of Shem
Genesis 28:10-15	Jacob, not Esau the 1st-born (type of Christ being the 2nd man/ Adam was the 1st)
Genesis 49:8-10	Judah, not Joseph, the 1st-born (same type as above)
2 Samuel 7:16	Line of David

Up to the time of Jesus, all Jewish genealogical records were preserved in the Temple: God always plans everything exactly right! The lineage of both Mary and Joseph were necessary for Jesus' lineage. Why? Since Joseph was the adopted father of Jesus, Jesus was from the kingly line of David. Through Mary, however, he was in the legal line of David – all as promised! Jesus' bloodline didn't come through Joseph's line, as told to Coniah.

+ Priests were required to produce an unbroken record of their descent from Aaron
+ Priests' wives were required to show 5 generations of their geneological records to prove they were of pure Israeli blood
+ In 70 A.D. Rome destroyed the Temple and all genealogical records

TODAY: The only person who can trace their ancestry back to David to show he has both a kingly and legal right to the throne is **Jesus**! His records are preserved for all mankind in the Bible!

123

The Theory of the Re-Creation

(Most of this information came from Clarence Larkin's book, *Dispensational Truth.*)

Genesis 1:1 states simply that God at some point created (made from nothing) the heavens and the earth. He does not take the time to explain to us how he went about this. We must simply accept this as fact, because it is the Word of the Creator. The word *was* in verse 2 may also be translated *became*. It often aids our understanding to look at several translations of the Bible to try to find what is closest to the original text.

The words *without form* are from the word in the original language, *tohuw,* which also is translated *in vain.* Literally, the original of Genesis 1:2 then states *And the earth was (or became) tohuw.* Isaiah 45:18 would read, ... *He created it not tohuw.* Could these verses be telling us the earth was not created a chaotic waste, but later became that way? Could God, who is perfect, create anything which is not perfect? If this is the correct interpretation, what happened to cause the earth to become *tohuw?*

Isaiah 14:12-14 tells us that Lucifer's sin was pride.

> How you have fallen from heaven, O morning star, son of the dawn! You have been cast down to the earth, ... You said in your heart, "I will raise my throne above the stars of God; I will sit enthroned on the mount of assembly, on the utmost heights of the sacred mountain, I will ascend above the tops of the clouds; I will make myself like the Most High." (NIV)

Ezekiel 28:12 – 17 tell us more information about Satan:

> You were the model of perfection, full of wisdom and perfect in beauty. You were in Eden, the garden

of God; .... You were anointed as a guardian cherub, for so I ordained you. You were on the holy mount of God .... You were blameless in your ways from the day you were created til wickedness was found in you. .... So I drove you in disgrace from the mount of God, and I expelled you, O guardian cherub, from among the fiery stones. Your heart became proud on account of your beauty, and you corrupted your wisdom because of your splendor. So I threw you to the earth; ....(NIV)

Note verse 13 tells us this being (Satan) had been in Eden before his sin and expulsion from God's presence. Job 38:6-7 tell us *all* of the angels were singing God's praises when God created the earth. So, this would include Satan before his fall.

From Ephesians 2:2 and II Corinthians 4:4 and the above passages, it is felt that Satan had an exalted position after the earth was created - a ruler of the kingdom of the air. When he sinned and was expelled from God's holy presence, the earth *became* a chaotic waste or without form.

Many feel Jeremiah 4:23-26 refer to this time of re-creation and others believe it refers to the end-time. Because of the verses above, I lean toward believing it refers to the time of re-creation. It is interesting to note the phrases *without form and void* and *no light*. God's first work was to cause the presence of light. Notice also the mention of *towns* in verse 26. Could Satan have ruled over these *towns*?

There's the possibility the earth could have stayed in this *tohuw* state for millions of years, allowing time for the formation of oil deposits and coal beds. The waters covering the earth in darkness would cause freezing - possibly an ice age. Maybe the fossils of large, strange animals (dinosaurs, etc.) are from the original creation. These are merely suppositions, because the Bible does not say, and it is the only word we can truly trust! But, the study of God's Word is so exciting!

I believe Genesis 1:1 refers to the creation of the original heaven and earth. It became *formless and void* after the fall of Satan and was then re-created for man in Genesis 1:3. Then we read how God restored the earth in the verses that follow.

Verse 2 says:

> *Now the earth was formless and empty, darkness was over the surface of the deep, and the Spirit of God was hovering over the waters.(NIV)*

It seems the earth was in darkness because of it being covered by water in the atmosphere. 2 Peter 3:5 says:

> … long ago by God's Word the heavens existed and the earth was formed out of water and by water. (NIV)

God called for light to penetrate this darkness allowing the light to be seen, so there was now *night* and *day*. He didn't create the light, so it apparently was already there. It just hadn't been able to penetrate the watery atmosphere before this time. This was the first day. Notice that God does not call this day *good*, possibly because the earth was now back to what it had been before the fall of Satan.

On the second day, in verses 6-8, God made a readjustment and placed an expanse (atmosphere or sky) and separated the water below the atmosphere from the water above the atmosphere. Again, God did not pronounce this day good. He was still dealing with what resulted from Satan's sin.

(We once had a discussion in my Sunday School class about why the Jewish days were "night and day" instead of "day and night." I believe it was because when God started His recreating, it was already night, and then He made the light appear. So, it started with night and then became day.)

In verse 10, we read that God separated the land and gathered the water and called it *seas*. He pronounced this *good*. Verse 11 states:

> Let the land produce vegetation: seed-bearing plants
> and trees on the land that bear fruit with seed in it ....
> (NIV)

This doesn't sound like He was creating them at this time, but they were *germinating* now that they were no longer under water and there was light.

On the fourth day, God set lights in the firmament – the sky. He placed the sun, the moon, and the stars. He stated they would be used for marking the seasons and time. The word *made* in verse 16 is not the same word as the word *created* in verse 1. That leads me to believe the sun, moon, and stars already existed before Satan's fall. Larkin states, *what is meant is that the clouds broke away and permitted the sun and the moon to be seen .... In other words, time* in contrast with *eternity* began.

On the fifth day, God created again. Apparently, all animal life had been destroyed in Satan's fall. God created fish and fowl on this day.

On the sixth day, land animals and man were created. Plus, God directed animals and man to eat green plants for food. In the King James version, God says *after their kind* five times in verses 24 and 25. There can be no doubt that they did not evolve from one animal. Besides, I have heard that when different species are crossed, the resulting animal becomes sterile. Also, man was created in God's image – not the image of an ape. This day he pronounced *very good*.

Chapter 2 of Genesis presents chapter 1 in greater detail. In chapter 1, God is presented as *Elohim.* - the creator God presented in His sovereign majesty. The facts are presented, but in chapter 2 more details are given. The name *Jehovah or LORD* is used showing God's character of love and concern. (In the New Testament, God is presented as *Adonai, Lord*. This term means *master*.)

I feel there is so much more we could learn in God's Word if we looked at the whole – dig through all of it instead of just looking at a chapter at a time, as we seem to do in this day and time. It feels to me we miss so much.

There are
so many, many
more fantastic
lessons in
God's Word,
the Bible,
so my prayer
is that each
of us will
continue to study
to find the wonderful
messages that God
wants to tell us!

Printed and bound by PG in the USA